GENERAL MOTORS

THE FIRST 75 YEARS

GENERAL MOTORS

THE FIRST 75 YEARS

BY THE EDITORS OF AUTOMOBILE QUARTERLY MAGAZINE

CROWN PUBLISHERS, INC. NEW YORK

PRODUCED UNDER THE AUSPICES OF GENERAL MOTORS CORPORATION IN OBSERVANCE OF ITS 75TH ANNIVERSARY
BY THE EDITORS OF AUTOMOBILE QUARTERLY MAGAZINE
IN ASSOCIATION WITH THE PRINCETON INSTITUTE FOR HISTORIC RESEARCH

AUTOMOBILE QUARTERLY PUBLICATIONS

Publisher and Editor-in-Chief: L. Scott Bailey
Executive Editor: Marguerite Kelly
European Editor: Griffith Borgeson
Associate Editor: Lowell C. Paddock
Editorial Assistant: Patricia H. Lincoln
Art Director: Michael Pardo
Assistant Art Director: David W. Bird II
Chief Photographer: Roy Query
Photographers: William Bailey, Richard Brown, Neill Bruce, Rick Lenz
Production Editor: William D. Clark
Business Manager: Kevin G. Bitz
Associate Editor for this Book: Barbara Long McHale

Printing by General Motors Photographic, Detroit, Michigan;
Binding by Macke Brothers, Cincinnati, Ohio;
Typesetting by Elizabeth Typesetting Company, Kenilworth, New Jersey;
Color Separations by Lincoln Graphics, Inc., Cherry Hill, New Jersey.
Copyright © 1983 Automobile Quarterly, Inc., Princeton, New Jersey, and
General Motors Corporation, Detroit, Michigan. All Rights Reserved.

Inquiries should be addressed to Crown Publishers, Inc., One Park Avenue, New York, New York 10016.
Published simultaneously in Canada by General Publishing Company Limited.
Library of Congress Cataloging in Publication Data
Main entry under title:
General Motors, the first 75 years.
1. General Motors Corporation—History.
2. Automobile industry and trade—United States—History.
I. Automobile quarterly.
HD9710.U54G469 1983   338.7′6292′0973   83-14318
ISBN 0-517-55169-1
10 9 8 7 6 5 4 3 2 1
First Edition

TABLE OF CONTENTS

With this book we present a seventy-five-year history of General Motors Corporation, as shown through the nostalgic and colorful prism of the past. A pictorial approach has been chosen to exemplify some of GM's most significant and memorable automobiles, trucks, buses and trains—transportation that is so closely entwined with the history of America and that of the world. Above all this anniversary book is a tribute to three quarters of a century of uncontested leadership in transportation design and technology. We were inordinately pleased to accept GM's commission to undertake this book.

Selecting the vehicles for such a historical overview was no easy task, for as early as 1929 GM offered the potential consumer as many as seventy-two different models to choose from. The numerical listing of annual automobile production given at the back of this book underscores again both the difficulty of the winnowing process and the massiveness of GM's achievement.

The colossus that is the American auto industry staggers the mind. One-sixth of the jobs in this country rely directly upon it. At the end of the last decade, the U.S. produced four times more cars than it did babies. America's millions of vehicles are driven over almost four million miles of paved roads. No community is independent of the truck and personal automobile. Trucks carry more than seventy-five percent of our nation's freight, while buses are in ever-increasing demand.

"The American," William Faulkner once remarked, "really loves nothing but his automobile." There is as much truth as sour hyperbole in this statement. The American's affair with the automobile has been intense and prolonged. It is said that there are more automobiles than people in Los Angeles. Lewis Mumford has argued that "the modern American way of life is founded on the worship of the motorcar, and the sacrifices that people are prepared to make for this worship stand outside the realm of rational criticism."

If we in America are anything, we are fascinated to the extreme by the automobile's changing forms and technicalities in its ability to perform to our personal satisfaction. The automobile has become an economic, psychological necessity. It is a virtual constitutional right to own an automobile, a part of the American dream.

Four-hundred-ninety-seven organizations and clubs in the U.S. and Canada are dedicated to the preservation of the automobile and its history. The Antique Automobile Club of America, the largest and oldest, has membership of forty-nine thousand. There are over two hundred thousand registered historical vehicles preserved as living testimony of the automobile to society.

As the world's largest corporation GM has one million holders of common stock residing in the U.S., Canada and eighty-four countries, three-fourths of whom own one hundred shares or less, institutions owning eleven percent. GM is also the world's largest single employer with over 657,000 employees world-wide.

On the seventy-fifth anniversary of GM we publish our first pictorial history, a special tribute to the automobiles of yesterday and today, in affirmation of our confidence in the leadership of GM. It is the history of a company dedicated to the pursuit of excellence, the production of the very best transportation at the most reasonable cost, the meeting of the consumer's requirements in an open, free and competitive market. For three quarters of a century, transportation that is dependable, safe, and economical has been GM's overriding concern.

To trace the history of GM to its beginnings, one must go back to a time when neither the terms "automobile" nor "United States of America" were part of our language. For the beginning of the American automobile is to be first found in the fertile mind of Oliver Evans, a young inventor in the Crown Colony of Delaware. His idea for a self-propelled land carriage was to challenge him for the rest of his life—and would eventually culminate in an American automobile.

He wrote: "There are witnesses living, to whom I communicated my intentions of applying my improved Steam Engine to propel carriages, as early perhaps as 1773. . . . " Delayed by the Revolutionary War he, like a handful of other visionaries of the self-propelled carriage, set aside his dreams but temporarily. Evans was to dem-

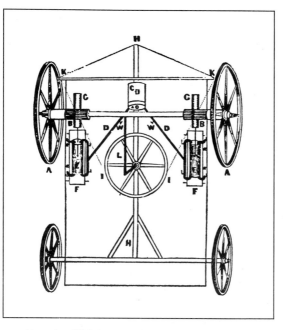

Above is a 1790 drawing of Nathan Read's land carriage. The two engines, one driving each wheel, would respond to the slower or faster movement of the wheels. One year later Read received a patent for a land carriage from the newly formed United States Patent Office. It was signed by George Washington and Thomas Jefferson on August 26.

onstrate his model, drawings and specifications on May 19, 1787 before the legislative committee of the newly formed Maryland House of Delegates. The House approved his patents and the Senate concurred two days later. Elsewhere at this time John Fitch, James Rumsey, Nathan Read, Isaac Briggs and John Stevens were also

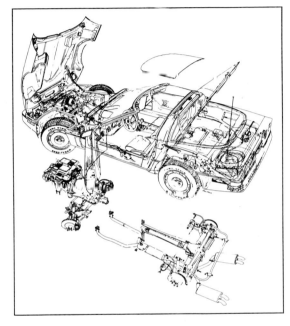

One-hundred-ninety-two years later is the 1984 Chevrolet Corvette, the most technologically advanced automobile ever produced by GM. The Corvette's twin computers process 300,000 pieces of information each second and its fuel-injected 5.7 liter V-8 allows it to accelerate from 0 to 100 mph and return to 0 in 22.4 seconds.

presenting plans for patenting self-propelled carriages.

For generations it has been assumed and endlessly repeated in books and encyclopedias that the automobile was European by birth and American merely by adoption. This *fait accompli* was severely and strenuously impressed upon me when, after receiving a Fulbright schol-arship to England's Oxford University, I suggested that my field of study be the history of the American automobile. Although my advising professor W. E. Smith recommended that I seek another doctoral topic, in view of my passion for the subject he graciously directed me to his close colleague Professor Allan Nevins, two-time Pulitzer Prize winner for American history, and a member of the faculty at Columbia University.

He likewise assured me that the soil would be barren for research until just before the turn of the present century. "There is not much to tell," he warned. "It started with the Model T. Certainly one could go no further back than the Duryea brothers' car that rests in the Smithsonian Institution with the date of 1893." His colleagues in England concurred. Seven years later Nevins published his famous trilogy on the history of Henry Ford and his company, an impeccable and important work that was the product of a grant by the Ford Motor Company. My turn would not come so soon.

It was not until ten years after the founding of *Automobile Quarterly* magazine in 1962 that I returned to my earlier quest. *The American Car Since 1775*, Automobile Quarterly's first book, was the partial fulfillment of my desire to record the history of the very beginning of the American automobile. Over one hundred self-propelled vehicles powered by electricity, steam, air and various explosive vapors were on the American roads between Oliver Evans' patent and 1891.

My interest in automobiles began not unlike that of any other young man who returned from World War II and wanted his own "wheels." But what started as an interest soon became an intense and prolonged passion that eventually led to the founding of a very unconventional magazine devoted to the automobile of today, yesterday and tomorrow.

During the past two decades we have been inordinately proud of our issues of *Automobile Quarterly* as well as the books we have published. High on our list are complete histories of five GM operations—Buick, Cadillac, Chevrolet, Oldsmobile and Opel. Then, too, there are our histories of Camaro and Firebird. Our other books cover an exhaustive range of automobile marques; as evidence of their widespread appeal, several have also been translated into German and Italian.

Appreciation must be expressed to the many who have helped shape *General Motors—The First 75 Years of Transportation Products*. A special thanks to Dave Holls, an esteemed and respected historian of automotive design, who also is responsible for GM's advanced design. With Dave we reviewed the selection of each automobile to be pictured. To Pierre Ollier a special thanks for his expert advice, not only about trucks, but about the great sweep of GM's automotive history. Thanks, too, to Thomas F. Macan of GM's Public Relations Staff. Of the many others at GM who have helped bring this book to print, recognition is due to Thomas J. Mullen, Edward S. Lechtzin, Ronald L. Herron, Donald J. Cislo, John G. Kolmetz and Guy C. Mellick. Thanks also to the Princeton University Library and most especially the vast and always growing National Automotive History Collection housed, albeit inadequately, at the Detroit Public Library; for without this outstanding reference source few books on American automobile history could be published. May the collection be more fully attended by the industry it so importantly preserves.

I am most appreciative of again being given complete access to the archives and personnel of GM, its divisions and overseas companies. Of course any errors which might have occurred remain our responsibility.

Finally I would like to offer special thanks to those who have made their cars available to us for photography. Through their long hours of research and faithful restoration, they have preserved a memorable aspect of GM's contribution to the history of the automobile.

L. Scott Bailey
Publisher

Princeton, New Jersey

CHAPTER ONE
THE AMERICAN AUTOMOBILE
1772-1895

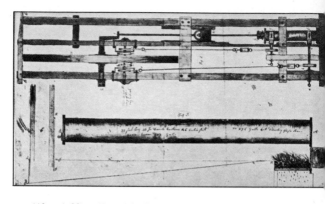

The automobile, as has been said before, was born in many places and at many times. What is disturbing is that so often the view is taken that the automobile was virtually nonexistent in America until it was introduced from Europe; that America did not develop the automobile idea, but merely borrowed it. This is simply not true. The history of the automobile idea can be traced in America through sixscore years from 1772 to 1895, the year in which an event clearly established that the automobile was in America to stay. The idea was rather revolutionary then, but so, too, were many other ideas about the new country, soon to be named the United States of America.

In 1908 the history of General Motors and of the American automobile became entwined and the two were to begin a unique pattern in the story of transportation. Formally chartered on September 16, 1908 in Hudson County, New Jersey GM quickly expanded to include numerous manufacturing companies—those of automobiles as well as ancillary organizations. In time GM would engage in the production of household appliances and other products. Yet originally, and ultimately, GM concerned itself with the manufacture and development of the self-propelled vehicle—the personal automobile, the commercial vehicle, the public bus, coach and rail locomotive. The story of the American automobile and GM is a microcosm of the history of the U.S.

Back in 1772, while Samuel Adams was inciting patriots to political action in Boston, Oliver Evans, a young inventor in the Crown Colony of Delaware, had an idea that would challenge him for the rest of his life—a dream that would ultimately become, through many hands, the American automobile. Evans could not shake from his mind hearing about a blacksmith's son who, after stopping up the touchhole of a rifle, filling the long barrel with water and stuffing the end with wadding, put the breech-end of the weapon into his father's fire to produce a shot as if loaded with gunpowder. Evans wrote: "It immediately occurred to me that there was a power capable of propelling any wagon, provided that I could apply it, and I set myself to work to find out the means of doing so." Applying the power would be the nemesis for young Evans and many others during the coming century.

Armed with drawings, specifications and a model steam engine Evans effectively demonstrated his principles for a road wagon before the legislative committee of the House of Delegates of the new state of Maryland, who granted him a patent on May 19, 1787. By 1792 Evans had built a reciprocating engine, both horizontal and vertical, plus a rotary engine and a boiler enclosing his furnace. He was working under the most primal conditions in a country as new as many of his ideas.

With the founding of the United States Patent Office all states were required to relinquish their patents to the jurisdiction of the federal government. Among the several to reapply was Nathan Read of Warren, Massachusetts, a Harvard professor, judge and member of Congress. His patent, the first for a land carriage from the new patent office, was signed by Thomas Jefferson and George Washington on August 26, 1791.

Read had gained an audience with George Washington and on April 23, 1791 had petitioned the Secretary of State, Secretary of Defense and Secretary from the Department of War for the opportunity to show that he had a "simple method of moving land carriages by power of steam." Read employed two double-acting engines, the pairing contrived to facilitate steering. But the new government declined to advance money to Read, and the visionary Read, embittered by rejection, would later sum up his work: "I was too early with my steam projects and

(Above) Oliver Evans' high pressure steam engine of 1802–1804. (Right center top) Evans' amphibian drawn 29 years after the event. The artist's imagination was wholly unequal to his task, the errors many and obvious. (Far right top) the third company organized to build self-propelled carriages and Evans' announcement of his demonstration 3–4 mph run. (Far right bottom) Roper's steam velocipede of 1869 on view at the Smithsonian. (Below) a model of Samuel Morey's 1826 gas and vapor engine on exhibition at the Long Island Automotive Museum in 1966. (Right center bottom) Drake's engine, with hot-tube ignition.

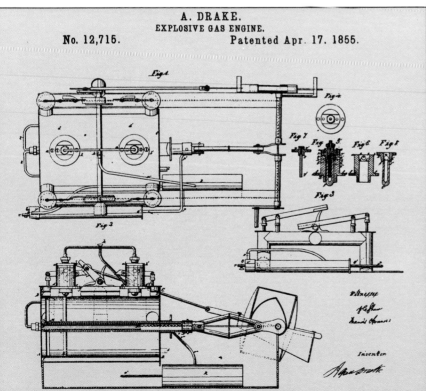

A. DRAKE.
EXPLOSIVE GAS ENGINE.
No. 12,715.   Patented Apr. 17. 1855.

the country was then too poor and I have derived neither honor nor profit from the time and money extended."

James Rumsey of Maryland and John Fitch of New Jersey, the first Americans to propel boats by steam, met with similar rejection. Fitch, a mechanical genius who was flawed by stubbornness, with an excitable temper and a panoramic range of personal problems, committed suicide in an hour of dejection after moving to Kentucky.

Oliver Evans continued to develop his patented high-pressure steam engine, which proved to be a boon to the development of grain mills and enabled him to become the foremost American millwright. His book, *The Young Mill-wright and Miller's Guide,* went through fifteen editions and a French translation. But the idea of a land carriage was never far from his mind, and on September 26, 1804 he presented the proposition of a steam wagon to the Lancaster Turnpike Road Company.

Evans also suggested forming the Experimental Company to go into the business of building steam wagons; he proposed selling 115 shares at $30 each to raise enough capital to build his wagons. His improved, high-pressure steam engine of 1804 had a 6 in. bore, 18 in. stroke and ran at 35 rpm with a working pressure of 50 lbs.

Commissioned by the city of Philadelphia to build a river dredge, Evans equipped it with wheels that would run 3 to 4 mph on land. He demonstrated it to prove the feasibility of building large, self-propelled land wagons capable of carrying 100 barrels of flour per wagon over the new 62 mile private pike in two days, for a profit of $50. This was a sharp contrast to five horse-drawn wagons taking three days and making a profit of only $18.30.

Colonel John H. Stevens, an important figure during the Revolutionary War, built his first steam carriage in 1802. His enthusiasm for a land carriage was boundless. One morning he had an idea for a new type of steam engine. Still in bed he used his fingernail to sketch its plan on the back of his wife, Rachel Cox Stevens, a woman of great beauty and good humor. When she started Stevens commanded her to hold still. "Don't you know what kind of figure I'm making?" he asked. "Yes, Mr. Stevens," she replied demurely, "—the figure of a fool."

After he determined that existing roads were too poor, in 1826 he completed a circular exhibition track near the present site of Stevens Institute in Hoboken, New Jersey on which to display his first steam engines.

Also in 1826 Samuel Morey of Oxford, New Hampshire built and obtained a patent for a gas and vapor engine, a two-cycle explosive mechanism with poppet valves, a primitive carburetor, electric spark and water cooling. Morey's engine is usually regarded as the most

Steam would find favor in the newly organized professional fire departments; the engine doing double duty, propelling wheels and operating water pumps. Fire apparatus remained horse-drawn until the 20th century. (Right) one of the first fire engines, Perry Dickson's of 1865. (Far right top) a New York City fire engine of the mid 1860's. (Below) Richard Dudgeon's 1866 steamer; he built his first in 1857 "to end the fearful horse murder and numerous other ills inseparable from their use." (Far right center) Sylvester H. Roper, early and prolific inventor of the steam carriage, on a pre 1863 model. (Far right bottom) an 1867 steam carriage designed and built by Henry Seth Taylor, a jeweler in Stanstead, Quebec.

successful American application of the internal combustion principle. However, the construction of considerable numbers of "steam carriages" seemed so likely at this time that in 1831 the U.S. Congress studied the possibilities of government support and regulation.

Many American inventors explored the potential of compressed air power, and its tantalizing possibilities still intrigue engineers today. Its major drawback, then as now, was its enormous development expense.

In the midst of the experiments with steam, gas and compressed air power, the electric motor would seize the attention of the land wagon builders. Inventive minds everywhere were charged by the concept of electric power and it was not long before someone discovered a way to attach an electric motor to a set of wheels. The first, in 1847, was Moses G. Farmer, whose two-person carriage ran on an 18 in. track. Next was the engine of Professor Charles G. Page of Washington, D.C. who used a 16 hp motor driven by 100 Grove cells and could carry twelve or more people at 19 mph.

Among the more persistent experimenters with the internal combustion engine was Dr. Alfred Drake of Philadelphia, who devoted 20 years, beginning in 1835, to this project. Though his approach was similar to Lenoir's of France, his engine ignited with internal tubes kept hot by flame rather than the jump spark used by Lenoir.

But it was the mechanical genius of Stuart Perry which eclipsed that of his contemporaries. As early as 1844 the New Yorker constructed an engine that was similar to Morey's 1826 effort, but used turpentine for fuel. This internal combustion engine was constructed somewhat like a steam engine, a two-cycle affair in which air and vapor were forced into the working cylinder by pumps instead of being drawn in by piston movement. Perry's 1846 engine was also "self-started" with compressed air. Surely it is an engine rightly identified as a milestone in the history of the American automobile.

The steam engine, easily incorporated into horse carriages, eventually became the favored method of propulsion. Between 1860–1880 the American steam car reached its peak of development. In the vanguard was Sylvester Hayward Roper of Roxbury, Massachusetts who began his experiments as early as 1859. He built about ten vehicles in two decades, the first of which was an 1863 four-wheeled steam carriage weighing 650 lbs. and having capacity for two passengers. It was powered by a 2 hp engine with a 16 in. boiler and a water tank. Coal for fuel was carried under the seat and the per-mile cost was estimated at a penny. Although only 15 to 20 lbs. of steam pressure were needed to operate the little machine,

as much as 60 lbs. were available.

During the velocipede craze of the 1860's Roper built a number of bicycles with steam engines, developing what might be considered to be the first motorcycle. His last model timed a mile in 2 minutes.

W. W. Austen, or "Professor Austen" as he later billed himself, displayed Roper's cars at county fairs and racetrack circuits. Austen's handbills touted "the greatest wonder of the world," promoting instead of its mechanical marvels the fact that the car could run "...noiselessly and unwarily 30 mph on the highways. It halts and turns deviously or proceeds at a funeral pace at the bid of its driver." Austen could always insure a sellout by pitting a Roper machine against a horse in a matched race around a track. The one-mile record was 2:20 minutes for a steam buggy, 2:37.5 for a horse and 5:20 for a man on foot. The results were not always popular, and in Anderson, Indiana a body of citizens greeted his arrival with a succinct description of what they would do if the horse lost. After some reflection Austen cut an opening at the end of the fairground fence the night before and capped his next day's victory by escaping to the police house before the enraged bettors could lay hands on him.

To the Canadian Henry Seth Taylor belongs the honor of having built the Dominion's first steam buggy, begun in 1865 and finished in 1867. Discovered in 1960 and restored by Anaconda American Brass Company, it is on exhibit at the Ontario Science Centre in Toronto.

Inventors searched constantly for something more practical and less expensive than steam. As delightfully bizarre a means of vehicle propulsion as might be imagined came to the fore—spring power. Frederick J. Forsyth of Bay City, Michigan has been credited with the invention of a spring-powered car, and similarly whimsical fribbles were patented and reported to have been demonstrated in Richmond, Virginia and Manchester, Vermont. Among the most successful—using the word lightly, of course—must be the spring-powered omnibus which carried ten people on a demonstration run in New Orleans in 1870. Employing eight springs formed of a steel strip 8 ft. long by 18 in. wide and 3/32 in. thick, each spring developed 2 hp, giving a grand total of 16 hp. A selective mechanism allowed the driver to increase or decrease the speed. The United States Patent Office was flooded with applications for spring-powered automobiles, and there were more than fifty recorded attempts to build them.

To stimulate land wagon development the Wisconsin legislature in 1875 proposed a reward of $10,000 to any Wisconsin resident producing "a machine propelled by steam or other motive agent" as a "practical substitute for use of horses and other animals on highway and farm." Thus Wisconsin became the first state to subsidize the car's development and the resulting test trials, held on July 16, 1878 might well qualify as America's first automobile race. The "Green Bay Machine," weighing 14,255 lbs. with 3 speeds forward and a reverse, challenged "The Oshkosh." With only one forward speed and a reverse and weighing in at 9875 lbs., it could run for ten miles without refueling. In the tradition of the tortoise and the hare, the Oshkosh covered the 201 mi. course in 33 hours and 27 minutes at an average and stately pace of 6 mph. But bitter disappointment is often the fulfillment of government promises. After a spirited debate, the legislature reluctantly awarded only $5000 to the builders of The Oshkosh.

Conscious of the public's frequent antipathy toward steamers and loathe to test their inventions on public roads for fear of incurring the wrath of neighbors, inventors were forced to try their vehicles at first light. Public ire was understandable, even if the real damage was often done by startled and runaway horses—behavior which led one entrepreneur to offer a stuffed horse's head for attaching to the front of a "horseless carriage."

Other inventors enjoyed the encouragement of their fellow citizens and families. Ransom Eli Olds, for example, was the member of a second generation of steam pioneers. Employed by his father's company, P. F. Olds and Sons, in 1886–1887 Ransom began to work on his three-wheel steam buggy; it was a cumbersome and crude model weighing 1200 lbs. In 1890–1891 he attempted a second steamer, a four-wheeler using the parts from the first, which he found to be unsatisfactory. The vehicle was sold in 1893 for $400 to the Francis Times Company, a London-based patent medicine enterprise, and shipped to the Times branch house in Bombay, India thus becoming America's first exported automobile.

In the 1890's electric power returned to challenge the steam and combustion engines, as inventors concluded that its simplicity would prove superior. While the steam car was relatively easy to build, one had to be a locomotive fireman to run it. And in dismissing the idea of gasoline, electric disciples preached, "You'll never get people to sit over an explosion." The team of Henry G. Morris and Pedro G. Salom built a series of excellently executed electrics, paving the way for the electric car as we know it. Their first creation was called the Electrobat; it was not the only electric vehicle of the era to carry a reference to the power source in its name, as the following names attest: Electricmobile, Electragon, Electropropel, Autovolt, Elecar, Electrola and Accelawatt.

Many patents had been awarded for the combustion engine, but not until 1872 was there a patent so promising that even the U.S. Congress sat up and took a second look. The patent was granted to George Bailey Brayton of Boston. Special hearings on the self-propelled vehicle were held, and "A Report of a Joint Congressional Committee on the Horseless Carriage of 1875" enthusiastically described "...a new source of power, which burned a distillate of kerosene called gasoline.... Instead of burning the fuel under a boiler, it is exploded inside the cylinder of the engine.... This discovery begins a new era in the history of civilization, it may someday prove to be more revolutionary in the development of human society than the invention of the wheel, the use of metals or the steam engine. Never in history has society been confronted with a power so full of potential danger and at the same time so full of promise for the future of man and for the peace of the world."

Brayton's engine was ignited by a mixture of air and combustible gas in a ratio of 12:1, but its patent made clear that the expansion of its cylinders was less the explosive force on the pistons than "a true pressure due to the expansion on account of the fact that the piston is at the very commencement of its stroke when the expanding gases begin to act upon it." The charge of air and gas was carried in a separate reservoir to be drawn when necessary. Brayton's piston was single acting, a radical step that eventually would be universally incorporated. While Brayton's engine was well regarded by the U.S. Congress, its application to land vehicles was viewed with great apprehension by local governments, who were reluctant to allow the "explosive" device to run amidst their populace. In 1873 Brayton's engine was applied to a streetcar and in 1879 an omnibus. The bus' first transmission was hydraulic; when that proved unsatisfactory, it was removed and remounted with a shaft projecting toward the rear and with bevel gear to drive a cross-shaft. The bus also had a friction clutch and reversing arrangement. But all was for naught, as the vehicle was refused sanction to run on Pittsburgh's streets.

By 1890 the combustion engine, tried and proven, awaited a combination of factors that would permit a successful building of a horseless carriage. The engine had been reduced in size and almost refined to the point of being reinvented.

Awarding credit for the first successful American gasoline powered automobile—that is, one that could be produced in volume and was basically reliable—presents a number of problems. The claimants are many, the evidence disputable. The brothers J. Frank and Charles E.

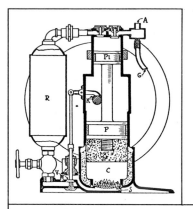

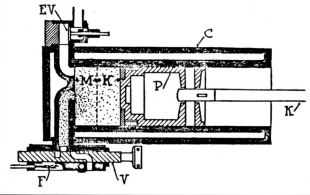

(Left and below) Brayton's 1872 engine. Gas and air were drawn from reservoir R. (Left bottom) Olds' second steamer of 1890–1891. (Right) 1895 Duryea patents for second car, filed by Charles E. though invented by J. Frank. (Right bottom) first Duryea of 1893–1894 displayed at the Smithsonian Institution.

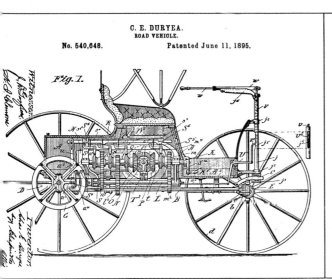

C. E. DURYEA.
ROAD VEHICLE.

No. 540,648. Patented June 11, 1895.

Fig. 1.

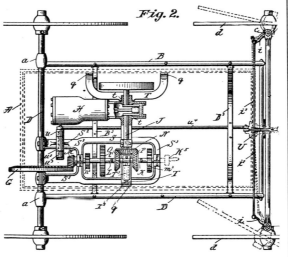

Fig. 2.

Duryea of Springfield, Massachusetts planned their vehicle in 1891. Its first run, made two years later, had been considered America's first until the 1950's when documents revealed that John William Lambert of Ohio City, Ohio could lay a better claim.

Another claimant is Henry Nadig; not long ago remnants of the vehicle which he built in Allentown, Pennsylvania were unearthed, and the car has been restored in modified form. Nadig and his brother built and sold gasoline engines in the 8 hp range, weighing approximately 1800 lbs. and averaging 5 ft. in length. For his horseless carriage, however, he reduced the engine to 300 lbs., beginning to build carriages equipped with this engine in 1891. Unfortunately the only documentation to substantiate this claim is Nadig's testimony during the famous Selden Patent trial of October 5, 1905. Interest in his engine revolves around the fact that in this single-cylinder engine, the revolutions were twice that of the countershaft in low gear and the same with the shaft in high gear, the ratio being 14:1 in high gear. This engine ran from 600 to 800 rpm, while a later 2 cyl. version attained an estimated 12 to 14 hp at 800 rpm.

There exist today several fascinating pioneer gasoline automobiles of mixed ancestry and sketchy documentation. One of the earliest is that of Charles H. Black; built in 1893, it is on exhibit at the Indianapolis Children's Museum. An 1892 Schloemer-Toepfer vehicle may be seen in the Milwaukee Public Museum. Both the Black and Schloemer-Toepfer were powered by a Sintz engine, a very popular American gasoline engine in the 1890's. Among those employing the Sintz was Elwood P. Haynes of Kokomo, Indiana who asked Elmer and Edgar Apperson to help him realize his ideas for a horseless carriage. Haynes quickly decided that the resulting vehicle, which saw its first run along the Pumpkinvine Pike on July 4, 1894 was worth manufacturing.

Conscious of the enormous publicity value of producing the "first" car, Haynes persuaded Lambert, who had previously developed a single-cylinder vehicle in 1891, not to raise a public protest when he claimed priority. Lambert lacked an ego sufficient to earn him a rightful place in the history of the automobile. However he would be honored as the originator of the gearless friction-drive automobile engine, and his patent credits for automobiles and other machinery were numerous. Lambert built the "Union" car, and later marketed a car in his own name, which would be produced until World War I.

Obviously there was no dearth of Americans who believed in the horseless vehicle in the early 1890's. They were to be found in the byways of prairie towns, the back

alleys of villages and the sophisticated machine shops of such cities as Detroit. What was needed was something that could bring together the tinkerers, dreamers and experimenters, an attraction of capital to further the development of their work, and public approval to assure its ultimate realization. What was needed was a catalyst. One might have been the World's Columbian Exposition of Chicago, which opened on May 1, 1893 to commemorate the 400th anniversary of the discovery of America.

The most impressive exhibit was Machinery Hall, where a Corliss steam engine supplied power for most of the mechanical devices displayed. More machine power was displayed there than had been assembled anywhere in the world; clearly, America had fallen in love with the machine. But where amid this assemblage was the automobile? There were a few, though visitors paid scant attention to them. Daimler Motoren Gesellschaft displayed a car, brought to the U.S. by American piano manufacturer William Steinway; also exhibited was a German Benz. Two electric horseless carriages stood in the Electrical Building. Except for these vehicles and the lone Sturges electric which carried passengers over the fair grounds for two years, the automobile was virtually absent, a strange occurrence considering that almost 200 patents had been granted to inventors of self-propelled vehicles powered by electricity, steam or a form of explosive gas vapor. Fortunately one of the exhibition's officials, H. H. Kohlsaat, was conscious of this omission and greatly disappointed.

Feeling certain that there existed the necessary machinery and skill to build self-propelled vehicles, Kohlsatt, the publisher of *The Chicago Times-Herald,* took up the cause. As a subscriber to some of the major European newspapers, he had read in *Le Petit Journal* an account of an 1894 race sponsored from Paris to Rouen; he also knew of the Paris-Bordeaux-Paris trek to be run in mid-June 1895. He became convinced that an automobile contest was exactly what America needed to rouse an interest in the horseless carriage, and as a good businessman, decided to combine the adventure with a circulation promotion project for his own paper. The event was to be held "with the desire to promote, encourage, stimulate invention, development and perfection and general adoption of the motor vehicle in the United States." Unlike the European events of this heroic age, his would not be a race, but rather a contest in which the question of speed was only one consideration. More importantly it was a testing, analysis and judgment of how to produce a substitute for a horse, intended to prove the superiority of the machine over the horse. It was to be international in scope.

(Left) 1891 Lambert. (Above) 1894 Haynes. (Below) 1892 W. T. Harris and William Hollingsworth bus built for the Columbian Exposition, but destroyed in a warehouse fire. (Right top) 1895 Electrobat II. (Right) Morris-Sturges Electric of 1890. (Right bottom) J. Frank Duryea, winner of the Times-Herald *Thanksgiving Day contest.*

After an initial run the self-propelled contestants were to be submitted to a series of engineering tests. A test rig designed to measure the motor vehicle against the horse and wagon in all circumstances was built. Eight vehicles appeared at the apparatus at the designated time, and preliminary trials were held on the last three days of October. The 75 to 100 manufacturers who had initially submitted their names had found that the rules and conditions required more time than they had anticipated. Accordingly the *Times-Herald* decided to postpone the event until Thanksgiving Day.

In the meantime, when asked about the future of the gasoline engine, Thomas Edison predicted that he did not foresee the industry of the future as being dominated by steam power. Then he was asked about his area of expertise, electrical power. "I don't think so," he replied. "As it looks at present it seems more likely they will be run by gasoline or naphtha of some kind. . . . It is only a question of a short time when the carriages and trucks in every large city will be run with motors."

What to call this discovery which was finally beginning to attract publicity throughout the U.S. was as yet unresolved. The *Times-Herald* contest promotion announced a second contest with a prize of $500 for "some learned and ingenious person who would coin a new name to take the place of that awkward phrase 'horseless carriage.'" On July 25, 1895 the winner was announced. G. F. Shaver, the general manager of the Public Telephone Company of New York, won with "Motocycle." The name would form part of the banner head for a new magazine to be published one month prior to the Thanksgiving Day event. Ironically this banner also carried the name by which the vehicle would eventually come to be known: *The Motocycle (Automobile) Maker and Dealer.*

On Thanksgiving eve eleven competitors declared for the 54 mile run, although in the chill morning light only six stood at the starting line. The Haynes and Apperson vehicle had swerved sharply to avoid a streetcar, smashing its forward wheel. Another team, the Baushke brothers, couldn't get their car to Chicago in time; while Max Hertel's vehicle suffered a broken steering gear. A. C. Ames and George W. Lewis were unable to get their vehicles running on that frigid day.

Thousands of spectators lined the boulevard along the route from Chicago to Evanston and back. The previous day's 60 mph winds had resulted in enormous snow drifts and the pulling down of many telephone wires on Chicago's outskirts, while the cold had rendered inoperable the many police alarm boxes. Ready to brave the slippery, rutted, snowy streets of Chicago were the Duryea motor

wagon, the De La Vergne Benz, the Electrobat II, a Roger Benz, the Mueller-Benz, and the Morrison-Sturges Electric. Absent was the long-reigning steam car. The contest began at 8:55 AM. Driving through the deep snow overworked the battery of the Morrison-Sturges Electric, compelling frequent stops to prevent the motor from burning out. As the cold air filled with the smell of ozone the Sturges vehicle was pulled off the course, the contest abandoned. J. Frank Duryea wound cord around the tires of his car to increase traction. Frederick Adams, who attempted to follow Duryea in a two-horse light wagon, insisted, "No horse on earth could have made those fifty-four miles through the slush and mud." Later he added, "To me this fact alone demonstrates more than anything else the great value of the horseless carriage."

When dusk had settled at 7:18 PM J. Frank Duryea, who had been driving for 11 hours, wearily raised himself out of his car at the finish line and was heartily congratulated as the winner. The Duryea wagon passed the technical tests with distinction. In reporting the event the *Times-Herald* concluded: "The progress of the preliminary trials has been watched by thousands of potential manufacturers in every part of the world and there is no doubt that there will be a great interest in the manufacture of these horseless carriages now that it has been demonstrated what can be done with them." The results brought instantaneous fame to the Duryea brothers. They won most of the early American auto races; subsequently, J. Frank Duryea won the famous London to Brighton Run of 1896, a victory the British still tend to sweep under the rug.

The *Times-Herald* race had brought together for the first time the country's automotive pioneers, many of whom attended the event although they were yet to build their own cars. It is generally agreed that the contest had advanced this country's automotive art by no less than five years and saved America untold millions of dollars in royalties; these would have been paid to foreign investors and builders had not the 1893 contest spurred the American pioneers to redouble their own automotive efforts. The contest inspired such future manufacturers as Alexander Winton, Henry Ford and R. E. Olds. Finally the American automobile industry was beginning. Barely three years after the contest more than 200 companies, capitalized at a total of $500,000,000, had been organized for the manufacture of motorcars; soon an almost equally large system of ancillary manufacturers was formed. If any single event can be identified as the catalyst leading to the ultimate acceptance of the automobile in America and the impetus for developing this new interest, that event would have to be the *Chicago Times-Herald* Contest.

CHAPTER TWO
THE BEGINNINGS OF GM
1897-1919

Charles E. Duryea said the *Chicago Times-Herald* Contest of 1895 only demonstrated that although the horseless vehicle was a promising mode of transportation, it would remain the toy of the rich and a challenge to sportsmen until it could "compete with the horse in every way." When a buggy and horse could be fetched for under $500 and yearly board for $180, the turn-of-the-century automobile was untried, notoriously undependable and—at two and three times the price—unconvincing. In the language of today it lacked credibility.

Olds Motor Vehicle Company was one of the many concerns aimed at the wealthy automobile buyer. Organized in 1897 the company built 11 different models in a two-year period. Powered by gasoline and electricity they all shared a high price tag. While company executives debated where to concentrate their efforts, a fire that ravaged their well-equipped facilities in 1901 made their decision for them.

Before the roof collapsed timekeeper James Brady had time to push only one car—a low-cost, experimental, gasoline model—out of the burning building. This salvage of a rejected vehicle became more than the Olds Company's salvation. Out of the chaos came the inevitable decision to build the famed, one-cylinder, curved dash model of song and memory. The "Merry Oldsmobile" would benefit both Olds and the automobile industry as a whole.

The results demonstrated, for the first time, the potential of a mass market for a low-priced car. The Olds curved dash would engender the rudiments of assembly line production, encouraging considerable, if wary, investment capital. The company's rolls were replete with the names of men who would create and guide the American automobile during its seminal years. The car's price was horse-trading level—only $650.

By 1904 more than 12,500 Olds curved dashes had been sold, pitting the ticking clock against the horse. Cadillac Automobile Company and Buick Manufacturing Company had been organized in Detroit in 1902, and by 1904, Cadillac's production was second to Oldsmobile's. Meanwhile Buick floundered, only completing 37 automobiles in 1904.

Then "the king of carriage makers," William Crapo Durant, took control of Buick. Walter Chrysler, among others, would insist that Durant "could charm a bird right down out of the tree," and by 1907, the charismatic new leader made Buick the second largest and most influential automobile manufacturer in the country. Predicting that "a million cars a year would someday be in demand," Durant began to organize a network of suppliers and producers similar to the one that had built his Dort-Durant Company into the largest coach builder in the U.S.

On September 16, 1908 in Hudson County, New Jersey Durant filed incorporation papers for the General Motors Company. By the following November Buick and Olds joined GM, with Oakland and Cadillac following in 1909. The heart of GM had been implanted in the automobile industry; Chevrolet, the missing artery, would be added in 1918. Between 1910 and 1920 more than 30 companies would come under the GM holding company. Among them were Welch, Ewing, Randolph, Marquette, Rapid, Reliance, Scripps-Booth, Sheridan, the McLaughlin Motor Company and a 60% interest in Fisher Body. GM Export Company was established in 1911 to sell GM products overseas. By 1920 GM offered a line of seven automobiles, a truck company and a group of supporting companies, including Champion Spark Plug, DELCO, Hyatt Roller Bearing, Dayton Wright Airplane and Harrison Radiator.

In 1901 Olds Motor Works planned to market the lineup of gasoline and electric vehicles pictured outside of its three-story factory in Lansing, Michigan.

OLDSMOBILE

The jaunty, 7 hp, 1 cyl. Olds curved dash quickly caught the public's fancy through publicity-provoking events and pragmatic advertising: "Nothing to watch but the road." A simple press of the foot was all that was needed to determine "whether your machine shall go at a snail's pace or at varying speeds limited only by your desires." That is if your desires didn't exceed twenty miles an hour! Five quarts of gasoline would last 50 miles, and 12 men could put their weighty 2100 lbs. on the little motorcar "without injurious effect."

Roy Chapin, on October 27, 1901, after being given a box of spare parts and a handshake and wished Godspeed, set off from Detroit to drive to the New York Auto Show. Seven days later, muddied and bedraggled, he arrived to be adulated by the press. Later a Manhattan dealer took orders for almost a thousand curved dashes.

Ransom Olds eagerly accepted a motor race challenge from Alexander Winton, America's foremost racer of gasoline cars. In April 1902 Winton and Olds met on Ormond-Daytona Beach, bringing Olds the distinction of being the first American racer to run on the sands of the "Birthplace of Speed." Olds' 1 cyl. "Pirate" and Winton's 4 cyl. "Bullet I" both clocked 57 mph. In 1903 Olds' 2 cyl. "Flyer" set a world's speed record of 54.38 mph for "light gasoline vehicles under 1000 pounds," and 42 sec. for a kilometer.

The majestic Oldsmobile Limited (below, 1910) was forever immortalized in "Setting the Pace," a famous painting by William H. Foster, the artist renowned for his illustration of the New York Central's record-setting run. Limiteds of 1911 had whopping 707 cu. in., 60 hp, 6 cyl. engines, wheelbase options of 130 and 138 in., with 42 in. wheels necessitating a double-step running board. They could easily cruise at speeds of 60–70 mph. A 1912 Oldsmobile Autocrat Speedster, a 4 cyl., 40 hp model (left) averaged 60 mph for 265.44 miles in the Long Island Vanderbilt Cup race, entered by a private owner only 14 days after purchase. (Above) 1908 Oldsmobile Model M Palace Touring car.

BUICK

David Dunbar Buick, Eugene C. Richard and Walter Marr share collective, if unequal, credit for developing the valve-in-head engine, a revolutionary principle that was eventually adopted by the entire automobile industry. The 2 cyl., 159 cu. in. engine developed 16.2 hp at 1200 rpm and 21.0 hp at 1230 rpm.

Before becoming infatuated with the automobile Buick built stationary and marine engines of considerable international reputation. He built three cars in Detroit before moving to Flint, where his lack of managerial ability caused him to be overwhelmed by debt. His fleeting but genuine success lives on in the name of one of the oldest and most revered of American marques.

Buick had succeeded in building between two and three dozen cars before William Durant assumed full responsibility for the company in 1904. Within two months he demonstrated the same salesmanship that had already made him a fortune in carriages, taking orders for 1108 Buicks at the New York Auto Show.

The Buick valve-in-head engine was refined to the point that it produced the power to out-climb and out-speed any vehicle in its class. Buick was the bedrock upon which Durant began to build GM.

By 1908 Buick's production had risen to 8820; it almost doubled the next year and soared to 30,525 in 1910. Top-of-the-line this year was the company's first closed car, the Model 41. The sumptuous limousine utilized a 318 cu. in., 4 cyl. engine. Meanwhile the range of Buick trucks became more diversified.

The 1905 Model C Tourer (above) and 1906 Model G (below), with a steering wheel that moved forward for easy entry, were powered by a 2 cyl. engine. The latter, although advertised at 22 hp, was rated at 27.7 in actual tests. (Right, 1910) One of the famous Buick Bugs driven by Louis Chevrolet and teammate Bob Burman, who took the title "World Speed King" from Barney Oldfield. Burman's Buick set a 105 mph record at the Indianapolis Speedway's 1910 opening.

In the decade 1910–1919 Buick met with increasing overseas recognition. An Argentine Buick dealer claimed in 1914 to be the first to drive a car across South America, taking a 1912 Model 28 from Buenos Aires to Santiago. A total of 1544 B-25 model chassis alone were exported; most went to England, where Bedford bodies were mounted, others were sent to the Abadal Company of Barcelona for custom coach work. The company's house organ published photos and reports of exotic events and personalities: a hill-climb victory in South Africa, a victorious tug-of-war with an elephant and the Sultan of Johore with his Buick. (Above) 1910 Model 17 Racer. (Below) 1915 Roadster. (Left) 1918 E-6-45.

CADILLAC

From its inception the Cadillac has symbolized the highest possible quality, a reputation that originated with one of the company's founders Henry Martyn Leland. Early and unique to the automobile industry was Leland's insistence on precision manufacturing. Every part was submitted to a limit gauge test. Everything down to the humblest grease cap had to be standardized and interchangeable with absolutely no reworking to fit. Consequently Cadillac's manufacturing tolerances would not be surpassed elsewhere in the industry for decades.

The general limit was set at one-thousandth of an inch, and in some cases reduced to half this figure. As Leland would say, "It is the foreman's place to know that every piece of work turned out by his department is RIGHT, and it is his work to teach his men how to make it RIGHT. It doesn't cost as much to have the work done RIGHT the first time as it does to have it done poorly and then hire a number of men to make it right afterward."

Named to honor the French explorer Antoine de la Mothe Cadillac, who had established in 1701 the Ville d'Etroit ("village of the straits"), the Cadillac Automobile Company was organized on August 22, 1902. The first car was undertaken in September and completed on October 17. It was sold and shipped to Buffalo, New York; the second car went to Chicago. When the company exhibited at the January 1903 New York Automobile Show, 2286 ten-dollar deposits on orders were received by mid-week, and Cadillac announced "sold out," achieving one of the greatest sales coups of the era.

Production of the Model A Cadillac (above) began in March 1903. Available with runabout body or rear entrance tonneau, from the exterior it closely resembled the Ford Model A, both cars having received Henry Leland's touch, while being mechanically quite different. The important difference was the precision of manufacture. It permitted Leland's revolutionary concept of interchangeable parts, making possible the automobile industry's incredible growth.

Named for the Seminole Indian chief the 1905 Osceola (right top) proved the feasibility of closed cars. (Left) 1907 Model K. (Right bottom) disassembled Cadillacs during RAC standardization test.

DEWAR TROPHY

Unique to Cadillac was its early technology of standardized part interchangeability. In 1909 Cadillac captured Britain's Dewar Trophy, the Nobel Prize of the automobile industry. On February 28, 1908 eight Cadillacs had been shipped to London. After being driven 50 mi., three cars were randomly selected and driven 23 mi. to Brooklands Motordome. There followed a severe test intended to disprove America's claim to automotive supremacy.

Members of the Royal Automobile Club oversaw the trio's dismantling. The 721 parts from each car were mixed and 89 off-the-shelf parts added. Given only basic tools Cadillac mechanics reassembled the cars. They were then driven 500 miles at full speed to earn the sobriquet "Standard of the World" and to win the trophy in which young Wilfred Leland Jr. posed for a memorable photo (top).

While various mechanical and electrical starters had been in use, they were large, bulky and inefficient. In 1910 Henry Leland's friend was fatally struck by a flying crank handle. A grief stricken Leland insisted on finding a safe self-starter. Cadillac engineers and Charles F. Kettering not only solved this problem but ignition and electrical as well as lighting ones.

The self-starter, manufactured by DELCO, was introduced on 1912 Cadillacs to become a universal system. By 1916 98% of American cars would feature a DELCO electric self-starter. After studying the record of 1000 stops and starts in new Cadillacs, the Royal Automobile Club awarded Cadillac the Dewar Trophy for the starter and electrical system. Cadillac was the only company to win the award twice. Its leadership in engineering reached further heights in 1915 with the first commercially successful, mass-produced V-8 engine and new transmission. Also new was the tilt-beam safety headlight.

(Left top) 1912 "Thirty" Coupe. (Above) 1913 "Thirty" Roadster. (Left bottom) 1915 "center door" Series 51 Tourer. (Right) 1916 Series 53 Tourer. Both the 1912 Coupe and the 1915 Tourer featured corner curved glass.

28

OAKLAND

Oakland, named for the Michigan county in which the car was manufactured, produced a wide and varied range of models. As GM's high-priced motorcar it competed with Cadillac, having but briefly a V-8 engine. Fewer than half a dozen early examples of this marque are known today.

(Left) 1908 Model A 2 cyl. Runabout with a wheelbase of 96 in. and a weight of 1600 lbs.

(Below) 1912 Model 33 Roadster, having an Ackerman Torpedo Windshield with fabric between the cowl and windshield, kerosene side lights, and Prestolight headlamps.

In 1909 the Oakland Motor Car Company united with Oldsmobile and Buick under the umbrella of GM. But two years before this merger, at the end of 1907, the first Oakland car was already related, in a curious way, to the other marques. Alanson P. Brush had been the assembly inspector for the 2000 engines and transmissions built by Henry Leland for the Olds curved dash. Afterwards Brush went on to become chief engineer for Leland's newly organized Cadillac Automobile Company, designing and patenting its earliest engines.

Fortified by his success Brush opened his own engineering laboratory and was sought out by Edward M. Murphy, a successful carriage maker from Pontiac, Michigan. Brush became responsible for the complete design of the first Oakland—built by Murphy's Pontiac Buggy Company—a relatively light car with a 96 in. wheelbase and a 159.1 cu. in., 2 cyl., vertical engine. Cylinder heads were of the screw-in type; the pistons moved up and down in unconventional unison, balanced through the use of a counter-rotating weighted shaft to produce 20 hp.

The Model K, Oakland's first 4 cyl., became a popular car primarily on the basis of its superior hill-climbing ability. Its production increased from 491 units in 1909 to 4639 units in 1910.

Oakland soon lost the services of Brush and Murphy; the former establishing his own company, the latter, prior to an untimely death, joining William Durant at GM. Despite this erosion of talent Oakland managed to produce 2000 cars in a two-year period. In 1912 it placed eighth in sales in the industry. A year later Oakland introduced its first 6 cyl., along with a fast 4 cyl. that was equipped with a self-starter.

GMC

Early concepts for self-propelled vehicles, 100 years or more before their advent late in the 19th century, were not for personal transport but to replace the hauling power of six or more horses. The very word "truck" is of ancient Greek derivation—*trokhus,* a wheeled vehicle for carrying heavy loads. It came to define a heavy, horse-drawn wagon. When early automobile chassis were adapted to commercial use, "motor" was prefixed to "truck" to distinguish the self-propelled from the horse-drawn wagon. "Truck" and "trucking" have come to embrace a multiplicity of commercial vehicles, a gigantic industry vital to American life.

Buick embarked upon the building of trucks early in 1910. Early Oldsmobile, Cadillac and Oakland trucks, among others, were often derived from passenger car chassis. But as a rule automobile chassis, with their light frames, engines and transmissions, were not suitable for heavy payloads. This led independent truck builders to develop stronger, slower and more powerful chain-drive gasoline engines as well as electric motors capable of hauling five and six tons. Two such companies, the Rapid Motor Vehicle Company founded in 1904 in Detroit and the Reliance Motor Company of Owosso, Michigan started in 1902, were represented by GM sales forces and subsequently consolidated with GM in 1911 to form General Motors Truck Company at Pontiac, Michigan. The new company was created specifically to build heavy-duty trucks and buses. GMC Truck & Coach Division came into being in 1943 when GM finalized the purchase of Yellow Truck and Coach Manufacturing Company, a merger of the GM Truck and Yellow Cab Manufacturing companies.

The cab-over-engine truck (left top) was built around 1911, and was the first to bear the GMC nameplate, today a famous symbol of trucking progress. While a simple cab was developed in 1908 as extra equipment, truck cabs did not become standard until six years later, when windshields first appeared. And it was not until 1920 that doors were finally hinged onto cabs.

In 1908 a Rapid model became the first truck to conquer Pikes Peak. Seven years later William Warwick set a transcontinental record by hauling canned milk in a GMC 1½ ton truck from Seattle to New York in 31 days of actual running time. The trip was to demonstrate the practicality of the National Intercontinental Highway, which proved muddy and surpassable only with difficulty. Roads and trucks would improve greatly, each supporting the other in the cause of better transportation.

The 1911 Model 2A ½ ton express truck (left center) was first built in 1910 and was Buick's first serious venture into the manufacture of commercial vehicles. It would be adapted to a variety of styles, including a paddy wagon, a motor bus and even a racing chassis. From 1910–1911 1859 units were produced. (Below) 1915 GM electric truck.

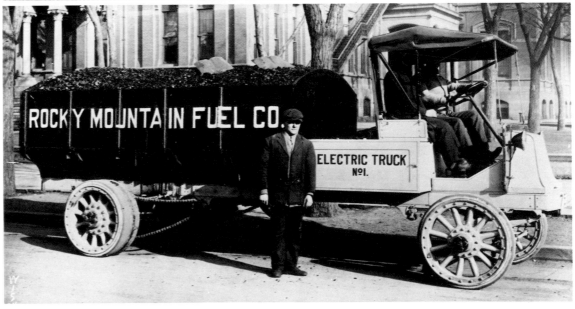

CHEVROLET

The first Chevrolet, the Classic Six (left), had a production run of 2999 in 1912. The Little Four of 1912 (below) sat on a 90 in. wheelbase, with an integral engine transmission and a 20 hp rating. Two 4 cyl. cars succeeded the Little Four in 1913. These new models, the Royal Mail (near right top) and the Baby Grand (far right top), were two of the first Chevrolets to carry in 1914 the "bow-tie" emblem Durant visioned. Whether Durant first saw the design on the wallpaper of a Paris hotel suite or in the rotogravure section of a Virginia newspaper is a matter of conjecture. A 1917 V-8 Tourer (right bottom) shows the beginnings of an integrated windshield with a noticeable highlight running from the radiator through the body.

During the spring and summer of 1911 rumors of an alliance between Louis Chevrolet and William Durant circulated in Detroit. Then, during the latter part of the year, Durant launched a trio of interrelated ventures, the Mason Motor Company, the Little Motor Car Company and the Chevrolet Motor Car Company. Although the companies' first cars—the Little Four and Six and Chevrolet's Six Type C Classic and Model H—met with an appreciative reception, it was the Chevrolet "490" with electric lights and self-starter that arrested car buyers' attention. The 490 was announced on December 16, 1914, shown at the New York Auto Show in January 1915, and placed on sale on June 1, 1915.

There were few adults in America who did not know that $490 was the cost of a Model T Ford. Within 17 days of putting the new car on the market the Chevrolet Motor Company had accepted orders, all secured by cash deposits, for 46,611 490s valued at $23,329,390. The 490 was assembled in franchised plants throughout the country to reduce costs and speed deliveries, offering a superior car to the Model T at a competitive price. During the summer of 1914 more than 1000 new orders were received every day. "A little child can sell it," Durant would boast. Six weeks after the 490 went on sale the Model T's price was reduced to $440.

In essence the 490 was the 4 cyl. Chevrolet stripped to essentials, put on a 102 in. wheelbase and offered in any color so long as it was black. A simplified version of Chevy's 4 cyl. 170.9 cu. in. Model H engine, the engine of the 490 developed 20 hp, the same as the Model T. In almost three years Louis Chevrolet and William Durant brought the company to fourth place in sales and by 1916 produced 62,898. Chevrolet became a part of GM in 1918 and during its first year with the corporation sold 80,434 "Wonder Cars."

WORLD WAR I

America's entry into the war unleashed the might of its highly developed systems of standardization and interchangeability which, combined with the advent of the assembly line and skilled labor, changed forever the concept of the permanent separate industry geared solely for military production. The automobile industry, with no previous experience in military manufacture, completed within only 18 months an outpouring of weaponry that is credited with the winning of the war, changing the face of Europe and giving rise to the U.S. as a world power.

The needs of the American forces and their allies were speedily supplied with the arrival of tanks, trucks, airplanes, submarine chasers, shells, ambulances, field kitchen trailers, airplane engines and a varied array of military supplies unthought of as the purview of automobile manufacturers—such as 820,000 steel helmets.

World War I was the first of four times in GM's history that it turned its facilities and experience to the production of war materials. Between 1917 and 1919 90% of GM's truck production was directed to war manufacturing, and the division sent 8500 trucks to the Armed Forces. Cadillac supplied 2350 army staff cars, 1157 artillery tractor V-8 engines, trench mortar shells at a rate of 20,000 rounds a day, and a large number of specialized military vehicles based on the V-8 145 in. chassis that included America's first full armored car.

Throughout World War I GM continued to manufacture automobiles for domestic use. The corporation also added two automobile companies—the manufacturer of the Sheridan car of Muncie, Indiana and the Scripps-Booth Motor Company—as well as the three Dayton companies of Charles Kettering, who developed the bomb-carrying, pilotless airplane. By Armistice Day domestic automobile production had fallen to 45%, and a backlog of half a million sales loomed for the postwar boom years, a period of short supply and nation-wide economic adjustment to peacetime conditions.

One of the corporation's chief postwar programs was the establishment of the opportunity to purchase automobiles and trucks on the installment plan. General Motors Acceptance Corporation, during its first year in 1919, enabled two million people to buy new vehicles. By 1925 three out of every four cars would be purchased using the installment plan.

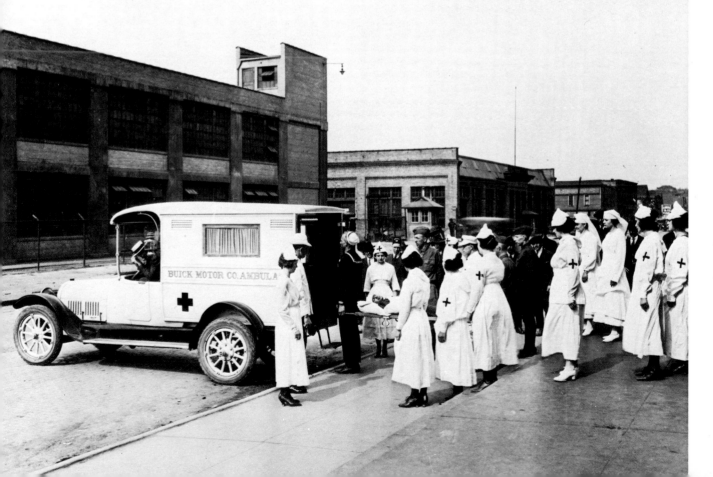

Manufacture of the 8 and 12 cyl. Liberty aero engines was a joint effort by the American automobile industry, with Cadillac and Buick dividing GM's share of the production. At the Buick factory (far left corner), camshafts were fitted to one of the 1338 Liberty engines made by the division.

Buick's war effort also involved production for Britain, including power and driving units for military tractors and military tanks, of which only a few experimental models were built. In 1918 Walter Marr is said to have worked seven straight days, with less than two hours of sleep a night, on an idea for a tank which was approved by Thomas A. Edison and other engineers. The completed vehicle was tested on the immense coal piles in Buick's factory yards (far left bottom).

News of the Cadillac V-8 and the outbreak of war were reported almost simultaneously. In the summer of 1917 the War Department tested several American automobiles in a 2000 mi. run. The Cadillac V-8 touring car emerged superior, and after completing another 5000 mi. test, was chosen as the standard army model for war use. A special closed car (far left top) was built in 1919 for General John J. Pershing, commander-in-chief of the U.S. Expeditionary Force to Europe. (Far left center) one of Cadillac's armored vehicles.

Perhaps the most famous single unit Buick produced during World War I was an ambulance. Serving the Allied wounded from 1914 to 1917, the Buick ambulance (near left top) was captured by the Germans, only to be retaken in 1918 by American forces. The battered vehicle was awarded the Croix de Guerre by the French government and eventually returned to the U.S. to be placed in the Red Cross Museum in Washington, D.C.

Production of Buick's Model 16AA military ambulances reached 50 per day. Later they provided a design pattern for civilian trucks. (Left bottom) a practice drill with Buick ambulance during World War I.

(Left top) a Buick experimental armored car in New York.

CHAPTER THREE
THE EARLY YEARS OF GM
1920-1929

In the years after World War I the automobile was firmly established. No longer was it a question whether the automobile would be accepted, but rather what kind of cars the public would buy. The 1920's witnessed GM's vast expansion, bringing a totally new concept of manufacture and management to accommodate the growing interest in lighter, less expensive cars to be driven for a shorter period and then traded in for models offering greater comfort, improved features and engineering advances.

The annual modifications, embracing changing public tastes and new advances in engineering, required high volume and great strides in research to economically fulfill GM's goal of producing "the best car for every purse and purpose." The annual model modifications changed GM and the manner in which cars were built and sold. They also created a second market, the used car, which provided more cars to a larger portion of the populace than ever before and at a lesser cost than a new car. Throughout this decade GM would develop a completely new system of management to address the problems of coordinating a decentralized and highly complex enterprise. The new management system would be adopted by other industries throughout the world.

The key to GM's success would be the research, development and testing of products well in advance of buyers' needs. Among the most significant accomplishments of the period was the development of Duco lacquer, an exterior body paint that gave richer, longer-lasting colors and reduced drying time from 336 to 13½ hours, a figure that was subsequently decreased to minutes. Prior to Duco a production run of 1000 cars per day required 21 acres of covered space that held 18,000 cars in the drying and finishing stages which required an average of three weeks.

Other achievements of the 1920's included chromium plating, crankcase ventilation, Durex bearings, automatic engine temperature control, Synchro-Mesh transmissions, engine-driven fuel pumps, hydraulic shock absorbers, reduced engine wear and noise, built-in heaters, automatic choking, four-wheel braking systems, numerous advances in body construction such as "V" ventilation at the base of the windshield, adjustable front seats, increased performance and dependability as well as continued advances in product manufacturing technology, resulting in continually lowered costs.

In the mid 1920's GM built the first of several world-renowned proving grounds to test automobiles, trucks and buses under all possible road and weather conditions. Also new would be a separate car products styling department, the first of its kind in the country.

These were also the years during which GM began its overseas operations. The first assembly operations outside North America were opened in Copenhagen, Denmark on October 25, 1923. During the same year Holden Motor Body Builders Limited of Australia began bodying GM cars. In 1924 GM Continental began operations in Antwerp, Belgium. GM's first overseas acquisition was Vauxhall Motors Limited of England in 1925. Assembly companies were established in France, Brazil, New Zealand, Uruguay and Sweden. At the close of this decade Adam Opel A.G. of Germany became associated with GM, eventually becoming the largest automobile manufacturer in Europe.

By the end of the decade a record-breaking 26,501,000 personal automobiles were registered in the U.S. This was only 34 years after J. Frank Duryea crossed the *Times-Herald* finish line in his one-cylinder to prove the practicality of the self-propelled vehicle, the long-cherished dream of several centuries.

Buick began supplying engines and components to Canada's McLaughlin Motor Car Company Limited in 1907, and signed a 15 year contract the following year. The resulting cars were known as McLaughlin-Buicks. Radiator caps carried the hyphenated name; hubcaps were often marked "Buick." McLaughlin became GM of Canada in 1918. (Above top) 1920 McLaughlin-Buick Tourer. (Above) 1920 Oldsmobile Model 37-B, sporting then-fashionable slanted windshield. (Below) 1921 Oakland Tourer. (Right) 1921 Buick 21-45 Tourer.

Charles Kettering's singular vision of a Copper-Cooled Chevrolet engine seemed to fulfill GM's quest for a low-cost, light-weight, high-performance engine with fewer parts and easy maintenance. While the new air-cooled engine had originally been intended for Oakland, scheduling pressures caused it to be released to Chevrolet instead. From its debut at the New York Auto Show, the 135 cu. in. engine, which developed 20 bhp at 1750 rpm, met with public indifference. The engine's realization fell short of its concept, and uneven air distribution throughout the engine continued to be a problem. The 1923 Copper-Cooled Chevy (left) is one of two surviving models.

GM's main-line truck was the durable K Series. The 1922 K-101 (near right top) featured worm drive and a dual-range gear box. The K Series trucks forever placed GM into the heavy-duty truck field.

(Far right top) 1922 Buick roadster with an English body. The one-millionth Buick, a Model 23-55 Sport Touring Car, was built in 1923. On August 1 of the same year the company celebrated Buick Day with exceptional enthusiasm.

Buick's 1924 lineup boasted a number of major refinements. Four-wheel brakes appeared after two-and-a-half years of research and 150,000 miles of road testing. The 6 cyl. engine was overhauled to give 50% more power: 70 bhp at 2800 rpm. Bigger on the outside and more roomy within, cars were given new styling appeal with a higher radiator contour—designed around a strong theme that was to evolve with many variations through the 1940's—high-crowned fenders and smoother and longer body lines.

Automotive Topics commented that the new Buick line offered "the purchaser a more aristocratic body than has heretofore been included in the Buick lineup" at a $50–$130 increase in price that Automotive Trade Journal called "surprisingly small." A total of 171,561 new cars were built, making 1924 the second-best year in Buick sales history. The marque was selling remarkably well, better than many cars beneath its price range, spectacularly more than cars above it. (Right bottom) 1924 Model 24-51 Buick Brougham Touring Sedan.

BUSES

Bus" is shortened from "omnibus," describing in French a public vehicle of large dimensions carrying passengers along a fixed city route. GM has long maintained a distinction between the terms "bus" and "coach." In 1925 it acquired the Yellow Cab Manufacturing Company, founded by John Hertz who painted his first taxis as well as his later tourist buses yellow. Hertz would later launch the Rent-A-Car industry. Yellow Cab and GM Truck became the Yellow Truck and Coach Manufacturing Company.

The big step in the evolution of the coach was the "Safety Bus" of the 1920's, which had a lowered center of gravity, an increase in engine power, improved air brakes and road shock absorbers. Although pneumatic tires as wide as 12 in. were developed during World War I, the practical roadability size became 10 in. Pneumatic tires were predominantly popular with bus and coach builders, giving a softer, cushioned ride. Later trucks would abandon the solid tire in favor of pneumatics developed for greater weight bearing loads.

By 1926 long distance buses were popular in California where railroads were not common. One year later it was possible to travel by coach to all major U.S. cities. A plan was underway in 1928 for a New York to San Francisco through route. For a short time GM developed a combination gasoline and electric urban trolley, providing freedom to depart from overhead electrical wires at various points.

Pictured are typical GM buses and coaches of the period. The 1924 Type X passenger sedan (near right top), commonly called the "Bob Tail Coach," was the last of the unique single door for each row to be used on a suburban route.

The Model Y of 1925 (near right bottom) is the earliest highway coach built by GMC, featuring a sleeve-valve engine, leather seats, window curtains, upper roof ventilation and exposed luggage carrier on the roof. Large hydraulic shock absorbers first applied to coaches, later to be refined for luxury cars, are evident in front.

One of the most remembered big city buses is the double decker with the top level open in summer and closed for winter. The first double decker built for the Chicago Motor Coach Company in 1923 was a 67 passenger and featured solid rubber tires. (Far right) 1924 67 passenger Model Z-67.

Buick

In 1926 Buick, for the eighth straight year, was given first-choice space at the Chicago and New York Auto Shows. This honor was awarded by the National Chamber of Commerce in recognition of Buick's top volume dollar sales. Dealers wrote over 15,000 orders during the first days of public showing, as unprecedented crowds mobbed their showrooms to see the all-new models. By June 1 Buick's total sales reached 1,360,259 cars—32% of all the cars GM had ever manufactured.

Buick's popularity rested foursquare on its reliability, performance, styling and low cost gained through high volume of more than 1200 cars a day. Prices had been reduced from $50 to $500 changing the question of "How can I afford to buy a car?" to "How can I not afford to buy a Buick?"

Engineering research and development, combined with endless testing on the new Milford, Michigan Proving Ground, would record the 1926 Buick as one of the most important cars produced by GM. The new models introduced some of the most significant advances. Horsepower was raised in the new Standard six engine to 60, in the Masters to 75. The Standard had a maximum of 70 mph.

Increased performance brought stronger components: strengthened disc clutch pack and drive line, transmission gears, axles and frames. An all-new oiling system filtered the entire supply in five minutes at speeds of 20 mph, a new centrifugal force air cleaner separated two substances of different specific gravity (air and water) to reduce abrasive engine wear. Heavier flywheels, counterbalanced crankshaft, torsional balancer, improved valve train and camshaft would later make a virtually vibrationless and superbly quiet engine. A winged goddess radiator cap replaced the motometer on the newly rounded modern-looking radiators.

(Right top) 1926 Buick Standard six Model 26.
(Right bottom) 1925 V-8 4 door Cadillac Brougham.

42

PONTIAC

Pontiac was one of the few companion cars that not only equalled but outsold and outlived its brother. Named for the chief of the Ottawas who ruled all the tribes bounded by the Great Lakes, the Alleghenies and the Mississippi, including the Deep South, the Pontiac was created to fill the gap between the Chevrolet and the Oldsmobile on the lower end of the pricing ladder. The Pontiac Six represented an amalgamation of engineering talent of Chevrolet, Oakland and Cadillac. Advertised as "Chief of the Sixes" it was introduced in January 1926 at the New York Auto Show; by July 23 more than 39,000 Chiefs had been sold, in 12 months 76,742. A year later it became the best selling "six" in America to rank seventh in sales. A remarkable feat for an introductory car offering two models, a 2 passenger coupe and a 5 passenger coach, with an all-new 40 hp, 186.5 cu. in., L-head engine with a 3¾ in. stroke—the shortest stroke then for an American production car.

Pontiac boosted Oakland's sales, and both outgrew the Pontiac plant. A new facility was built reportedly in 90 days, and all machinery was moved prior to opening day when 70,000 visitors were entertained. The building, sheathed in glass, was called the "Light Plant."

Pontiac also offered a ¾ ton closed bodied truck based on its passenger car chassis. With a payload of 3470 lbs. this truck would evolve into a GMC light-duty truck, Model T-11 and T-15A, continuing with the reliable six.

Pontiac was endowed with a forthright and spirited name, a modern look and many mechanical improvements. It was bodied by Fisher to make it a compelling attraction among its competitors as well as its brother. By 1930 Pontiac's bigger six option outpaced and outsold the new V-8 Oakland to become the fourth ranking car in sales. In 1932 Oakland production ceased, and the company was named the Pontiac Motor Company.

Chevrolet trucks have historically met with high favor among buyers of commercial personalized transport. Chevrolet built its first truck, a 1 ton, in 1918 and began producing its own bodies in 1926. (Left top) 1928 Chevrolet Series AB pickup. The 1927 Chevrolet Capital AA Station Wagon (right bottom) was an ancestor of the popular wagons of the 1940's.

(Near right top) 1926 Superior Model ice truck, with body by Hercules Corporation. Ice trucks would pass into oblivion with GM's Research Laboratories' development of the safe, economical refrigerant Freon and production of the universal "fridge"—the electric icebox Frigidaire. Over the years GM divisions and companies have produced a great number of advanced home and industrial products, some of which have found their way into unintended transport use. The logical step was a big Frigidaire on wheels for transporting perishable farm products.

Trucks and buses during the 1920's were undergoing change, and news-making stunts kept the GMC logo out front. "Cannon Ball" Baker filled a 1927 Chevy tanker (left bottom) with Atlantic Ocean water and drove 3693 miles to the Pacific in 5 days, 17 hours and 36 minutes.

One of GM's biggest trucks of this period was aptly called the "Big Brute." It exuded power and strength through a massive iron wraparound front bumper that looked like it could smash walls down, and probably could with its slow, powerful 415 cu. in. engine. Produced from 1925 to 1929 it represented the last of the boxy, bolted-together look. The new T Series of 1927 would have smoother lines and chrome radiator shells foretelling of the streamlining to come.

Buses looked as boxy. The 1929 Type W 21 passenger intercity highway coach (far right top) was built in a lowered chassis especially intended for passenger service, and powered by a Cadillac based engine. The "observation deck" concealed two spare tires, a design to forestall passengers' doubts of schedule when they viewed spares mounted on fender wells.

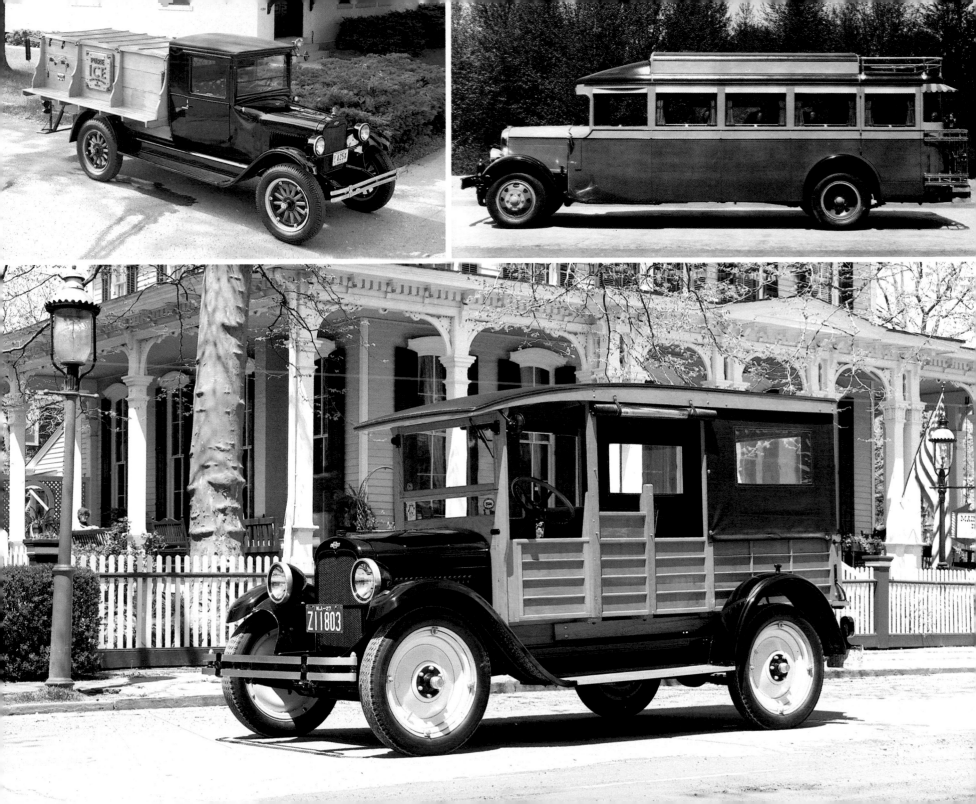

LA SALLE

The he 1927 LaSalle, produced by Cadillac, was the first professionally styled automobile to achieve success in mass production and was designed by Harley Earl, creator of GM's Art and Colour Section. Looking longer and lower with smooth hood lines and a high handsome radiator, it would set the trend for the American car toward the fleetness and grace of the Classic Era.

The LaSalle would also make important contributions to Cadillac's engineering history. It was one of three GM companion cars; the others being Buick's Marquette and Oldsmobile's Viking. Unabashedly advertised as "the blood brother to Cadillac" and of "Cadillac caliber," it was a high performer. It covered 951.9 miles, averaging 95.3 mph for 10 hours—an uncanny feat considering that the 1927 Indianapolis 500 was won by a 160 hp Duesenberg going only 2 mph faster for half the distance.

LaSalle's acceptance obliged Cadillac to build nearly 21,000 more cars that year than it had ever built for a model year. In the first three years almost 54,000 custom-bodied LaSalles carrying the reputation of Cadillac were sold. Continuing to benefit from Cadillac's sponsorship, reaping its engineering and styling advances, the LaSalles by 1937 and through 1940 were all Cadillacs mechanically, notwithstanding their superb, individualistic styling which caused a major marketing problem of distinctly defining the LaSalle's separateness.

In 1941 GM discontinued the LaSalle, replacing it with a lower-priced Cadillac model. The result was the greatest sales year in Cadillac's history, proving the enduring reputation of the Cadillac marque.

The LaSalle was named for Rene Robert Cavelier de la Salle, who claimed Louisiana for France in 1682. Although LaSalles were originally powered by a 303 cu. in., 75 hp, V-8, figures gradually increased to 340 cu. in. and 125 hp. Through the years the LaSalle shared many Cadillac features, including Synchro-Mesh transmission, dual independent braking systems and Knee-Action suspension. (Above) 1928 Cadillac Series 341-A Sports Phaeton. (Right) 1927 LaSalle Model 303. (Below) 1929 LaSalle Model 328. It was the first GM "convertible" with glass side windows that could be lowered into the door, complete with weather protection sealing.

46

When GM's Art and Colour Section began to quickly transform all bodies to present eye pleasing forms, even the less expensive models took on a look of elegance with a touch of line and splash of color. The stylist would change car terminology as well. Oldsmobile's companion car, the Viking, introduced in 1929, had new body lines as well as a new V-8 engine, and the once "rumble seat" was renamed "rear deck seat." The Viking, like the Buick companion car Marquette, was discontinued by the surprise of the 1929 stock market crash that was unhinted during GM's highest car sales in history. Oldsmobile alone surpassed 100,000 units for the first time this year. (Left) 1929 Oldsmobile Deluxe coupe. (Below) 1928 Chevrolet National Series AB, with Fisher body. The 1929 Pontiac Landau sedan, or Landaulet, (right) had a collapsible rear quarter cloth top. All Pontiacs that year featured 1¼ in. vertical Marvel carburetors, 10 spoke wooden artillery wheels, and after April, new 200 cu. in., 6 cyl. engines.

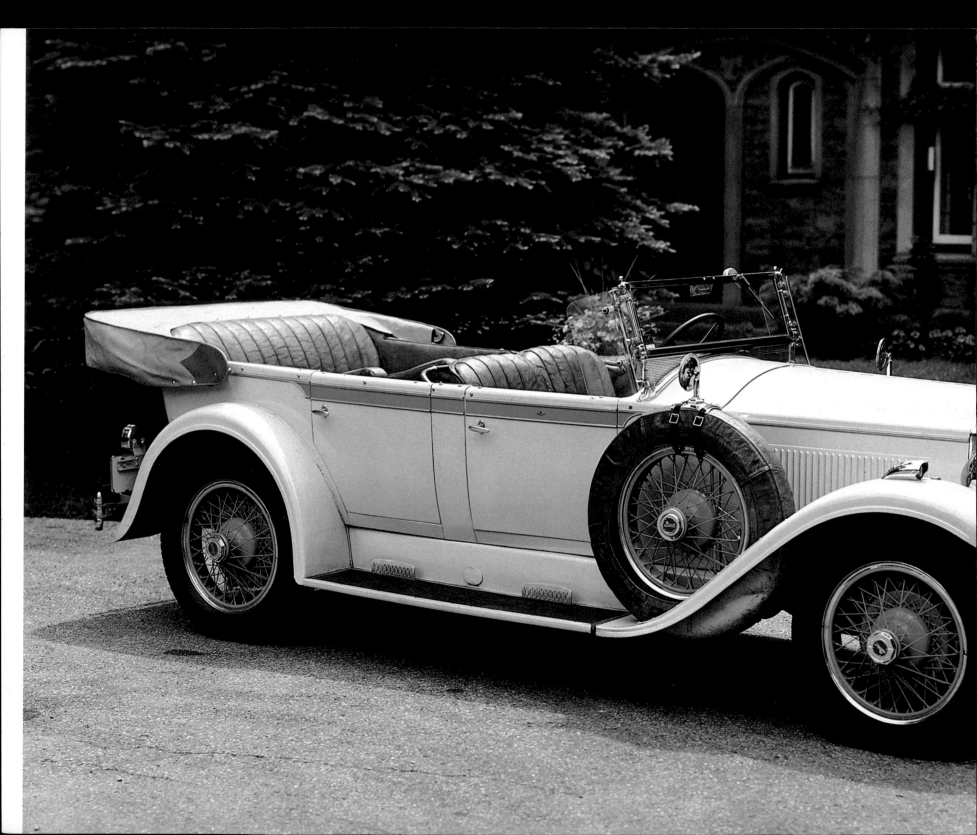

Canada's favorite car, the McLaughlin-Buick, was a joint venture between McLaughlin Motor Car Company Limited and Buick both before and after the formation of GM of Canada in 1918. It was also a popular import throughout the world. In England, where it was known as a "Dominion Built Car" and an "Empire Product," it was the choice of royalty. In 1927 the first of two special McLaughlin-Buicks were built for the style-conscious Prince of Wales. (Left) 1928 McLaughlin-Buick touring car.

To celebrate its Silver Anniversary Buick dealers invited their potential customers to view the 1928 lineup while listening to the newly available home radio. The anniversary cars' cylinder heads now incorporated spherical combustion chambers, increasing power and decreasing chances of detonation. Frames were double-dropped with deep side channels, reinforced with upper and lower flanges at the engine cross member and spring trunnions. Standard for the first time were the Lovejoy hydraulic shocks and the new Buick radiator emblems.

All anniversary Buicks were powered by sixes, but a new eight was in the wings for the beginning of the next decade. (Right center) Buick's 1928 Standard Country Club Roadster Coupe.

The best-selling six in America was the 1928 Pontiac. The Model 6-28 Roadster Coupe (right top) was endowed with a modern look and a score of mechanical improvements including four-wheel brakes and cross-flow radiator. The 1928 Pontiacs, with their narrow radiator shells and low body line sweeping from front to rear in an almost unbroken line, would set a new styling trend.

In 1929 Chevrolet, with a new valve-in-head, 6 cyl. engine, would again reach the million mark, holding first place in the industry. (Right bottom) 1929 Chevrolet AC Sports Coupe.

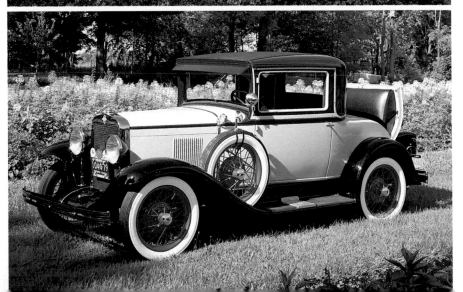

OPEL

In 1863 the soon-to-be famous German name Opel first appeared on what would become a million sewing machines. Later the gold oval would be in the forefront of the world's largest manufacturer of bicycles, producing at its peak 4000 a day. As could be expected the five Opel brothers, each a champion bicycle racer, quickened to the competitive aspect of the primitive horseless carriage. Teaming in 1897 with pioneer inventor Friedrich Lutzmann, they began what today is one of the four oldest and most honored manufacturers of automobiles to carry, with distinction, the original founder's name. In 1898 the prototype of the Opel-Patent-Motorwagen, System Lutzmann, was completed, and early in 1899 the first cars were offered for sale.

By 1910 Opel had built almost 5000 cars in an amazing variety of styles, each built piece by piece on sawhorses. Before World War I Opel had established itself on the map of Europe as an important maker of automobiles, a competitor in internationl racing and an exporter of trucks. In 1923, converting to assembly line manufacture and concentrating on one model for the entire line, Opel became Germany's first mass producer of automobiles. Painted green the 4/12 PS Opel was dubbed Laubfrosch—"tree frog."

The time had arrived when the Opel family wished to hold in their own hands the solid evidence of their skillful labors. In January 1929 Opel became a corporation, for which 60,000 shares of stock were issued, and at this time the present name, Adam Opel A.G., was born. Opel approached GM late in that year and by 1931 a merger was completed. GM's acquisition of Opel would be a new beginning for one of Europe's largest and most important manufacturers of automobiles.

By 1928 Opel's 8000 employees were able to turn out 250 cars a day. This was Opel's best year, with total car production at 42,771 units, and total car sales accounting for 26% of all cars bought in Germany and 44% of all the German-made cars that were sold in 1928. Such impressive facts and the international publicity of the Opel Rocket cars could not help but be noticed by the automotive industry.

Fritz Von Opel, an experienced war test pilot, became intrigued with flying a rocket-powered airplane, which fellow German inventors conceived as a stepping stone to space flight. Opel built three rocket (Rakete) cars in succession. Rak 1 reached 60 mph with only 7 out of its 12 rockets firing. Rak 2—also driven by Fritz on May 23, 1928—firing all 24 550 lb. thrust rockets reached 112 mph, the front end of the car lifting perceptibly. Rak 3, unmanned, attained 155 mph. On September 30, 1929 the Opel rocket airplane, essentially a wood and canvas high-wing glider with 16 rockets, was launched into the air by a rocket-powered carriage rolling on guide rails. Fritz reached 100 ft., firing 5 rockets before being forced down by a sudden gust of wind.

The first cars that were a product of the GM-Opel merger were the 1931 1 liter Cabriolet (right bottom) and the 1.8 liter (right top). The 1 liter, a 4 cyl. with an in-line engine, developed 18 hp and featured a pressure lubrication system, Solex carbure-tor and 3 speed transmission. The 1.8 liter contained the same features with a new 6 cyl., in-line, L-head engine developing 32 hp. At the time it was the smallest six and was said to resemble a scaled-down Chevrolet. The 1933 6 cyl. "Regent" (left bottom) introduced GM's Synchro-Mesh transmission to Europe. Produced through 1933 its curved body shape with clamshell fenders set new styles abroad. (Left top) 1933 6 cyl., two-seater sports car.

CHAPTER FOUR

DEPRESSION AND RECOVERY

1930-1939

The year 1927 marks the beginning of the modern automobile as we know it today. Designing the automobile was a modest activity until the advent of the stylists, under the leadership of Harley Earl, head of GM's newly formed Art and Colour Section. Together the stylists and engineers began to improve the appearance of the car and its components, giving attention for the first time to the general overall eye-appeal. The main concern was for a better proportion, more pleasing lines and a more harmonious blending of all of the automobile's components. The automobile would soon come into its own—no longer a vertical box suggesting immobility.

GM's stylists reasoned that the automobile was a machine of motion and should reveal that purpose with long, gentle and curving horizontal lines to suggest speed and power. Vertical obstructing lines would be shortened and square corners rounded. Lowering the car became a necessity to achieve a form in motion—a feat that was neither quickly nor easily achieved. Engineers as well as stylists at GM were proposing the basic change in the relation between the body and the chassis of the automobile. The step they took was the redesigning of the old frame into a new modern double-drop frame, moving the radiator and engine forward and solving the new weight distribution problem. However before the automobile could reach that point of design and engineering a great many steps were taken to attribute a more attractive line to the automobile.

Side windows, once all the same in the 1920's, were lengthened, their dimensions made uneven. Simply changing this area's proportions gave the impression of length, although the overall dimensions were exactly the same. Radiator hoods that merged with the body and accented belt moldings added further to the longer look.

The window lines were also lowered and the roof crowned. For the first time automobile fenders were given attention. The new ductile steels permitted graceful, sweeping, "flying wing" fenders with deep crowns adding to the longer and lower look. The V-shaped radiator, slanted windshield, fender skirts and body extension in the rear added greatly to making the automobile a distinct entity.

By 1935 the automobile had an entirely different look. The doors reached almost to the running boards and the apron had partially disappeared as a result of the lower frame. The back of the car now covered the gas tank, and the trunk blended into the body. The radiator was hidden behind a finely designed grille and the filler cap disappeared under the hood, giving a particularly distinct shape to the car front. Next would come the redesigning of the roof into a smooth, mold-free, all-steel top, achieved through stamping techniques and the availability of a wider steel strip, which resulted in the famed Turret Top developed by Fisher Body.

During the mid 1930's stylists started a trend toward streamlining the automobile. The plan view of the car gave the evocation of an object penetrating the air effortlessly, the body widening at the center of the rear doors tapering toward the front and rear fenders, tear dropping, and the running boards gradually disappearing. By 1937 the Art and Colour Section was renamed GM Styling—an appropriate designation in view of the tremendous changes brought about in the shape and look of the automobile.

Styling and engineering advances, made by both professions through their concept of the future of the automobile and the fulfillment of its purpose, would complement each other in the progress and development of the automobile in the future.

1930 Vauxhall 20/60 Boattail Speedster.

VAUXHALL

Vauxhall, an old and venerable name, dates back to the 13th century when an adventurous Norman soldier of humble birth, Fulk le Breant, entered the service of King John of Magna Carta fame. Through his grateful king he became Sheriff of Oxford and was granted the right to bear a coat of arms, choosing the griffin as his heraldic emblem.

Fulk married well, acquiring his wife's South London property, named Fulk's Hall. The property, eventually corrupted to Fawke's Hall and ultimately to Vauxhall, became in 1857 the site of the Vauxhall Iron Works. Originally a manufacturer of marine engines, the company built its first automobile in 1903 and christened it Vauxhall.

In 1905, the same year that Vauxhall moved to Luton, a 4 cyl. model was built. It sported a fluted radiator which, like the griffin, became a distinctive Vauxhall design. The 1911 C-type, later known as the Prince Henry, has been called the first true British-made sports car. The D-type model of 1912 was a popular touring car, accumulating reliable sales through the end of 1921.

When Vauxhall became a GM subsidiary in 1925 the name was as illustrious and as adventurously attributed as was its namesake. Vauxhall cars rivaled Sunbeams and did drummingly well against Austin, Morris and Ford. Vauxhall became the first 20 hp car to exceed 100 mph. Much of its reputation was earned through the skill of Lawrence Pomeroy, one of Britain's most famed engineering geniuses. Chevrolet's 6 cyl. engines paved the way for Vauxhall trucks, which later evolved into Bedford commercial trucks and buses in 1931.

Vauxhall's first commercial vehicle to bear the Bedford name, a 2 ton truck, appeared in April 1931, gaining immediate acceptance. Before the year's end Vauxhall began building buses, and by 1932 over 12,000 Bedfords were sold.

The 1931 Waveney-bodied WHB bus (left) was built on a modified truck chassis. Two designations were given to buses built on these chassis, the WHB and WLB. The 14 seater WHB was built on a 131 in. wheelbase, while the WLB, a 20 seater, sat on a 157 in. wheelbase. Both were powered by the same 6 cyl. engine as their truck counterparts. The first chassis built specially for buses appeared in August 1931. At the end of that year 52% of all 14 and 20 seater buses registered in the United Kingdom were Bedfords. The WHB was produced until mid 1933, while the WLB continued until 1935.

In 1925 GM purchased Vauxhall and changed the English marque's production emphasis from expensive luxury models to lower-priced family cars. The 1930 Vauxhall Cadet was the first product to reflect the new emphasis. The 6 cyl. model was available in a 17 hp or 26 hp version. The 1931 Cadet was the first British car to offer a Synchro-Mesh transmission. (Right center) 1930 20/60 Kingston Sportsman's Coupe.

Following the Cadet in popularity as well as production was the 1933 A-type Light Six (right bottom). Like its predecessor the Light Six offered two horsepower versions, a 12 hp and 14 hp. In its first year the 6 cyl. Light Six accounted for 40% of all 14 hp new-car registrations in Britain.

Through the mid 1930's, a time when a major economic depression was crippling most industries, Vauxhall was able to progress and expand. In 1934 production output had grown to 20,000 cars a year. By this time Vauxhall had also returned to the big car market, though not the high-priced end of it, with its Big Six models. Eventually special bodies were available on the Big Sixes. The 1936 Cabriolet (right top), fitted on a 12 hp DY chassis, featured body work by Martin Walter Wingham.

The very phrase "sixteen cylinders" implies something super excellent; it is suggestive perhaps of the sibilant whisper of the great engine itself. The 1930 Cadillac V-16 engine (left) was a classic in its own right like no other. With 452 cu. in. displacement, 3 in. bore, 4 in. stroke, twin carburetion, overhead valves and hydraulic tappets, the 45° V-16 was indeed the first automobile engine to actually be styled. The result of 16 years of V-engine development and experience it stood uniquely alone, the first of its kind within the corporation. It also served as a base for the smaller V-12. With silken smoothness, masterful quality and instant thrust of power, the engine was a marvel of engineering excellence. A total of 3878 overhead-valve V-16s and 10,821 V-12s were built from 1930 to 1937. From 1938 to 1940 a small run of 508 second generation V-16s were built. Unsophisticated in concept they were smooth, quiet and reliable. The 1930 Cadillac V-16 Fleetwood Roadster (below) was available in virtually unlimited colors, with chromium hood and cowl ventilators. A true forerunner of the 4 door convertible was the 1930 LaSalle (near right). The 5 passenger car called the "Fleetwing Sedanette Cabriolet" effectively combined the open look of a phaeton or touring car with the all-weather practicality of a closed car.

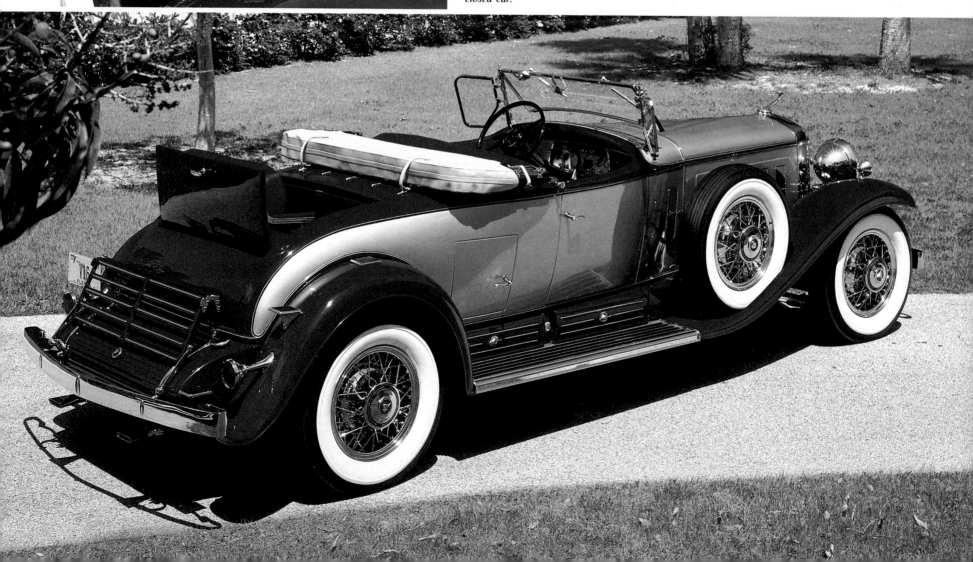

Marquette, the lower-priced "Baby Buick," was introduced on June 1, 1929, just weeks ahead of the new full-sized Buick models. Powered by a 6 cyl. L-head, a virtual carbon copy of the successful Oldsmobile flathead six, the Marquette lent itself to a lighter, more economical unit. When attended by Buick's engineering mastery, it achieved outstanding performance, durability, speed and riding comfort. The 1930 Marquette (below), built on a 114 in. wheelbase, was offered in six body styles with optional wire wheels and sidemounts. Its 212.8 cu. in. engine developed 67.5 hp at 3000 rpm, accelerating from 5 to 25 mph in 8.8 seconds with a top speed of 70 mph. A promotion run from Death Valley to Pikes Peak, 778 arduous miles, was completed in 40 hours and 45 minutes.
The 1930 Oakland sedan (near right) had a new V-8 engine identical to the valve-train design of the 1929–1930 Olds Viking. The Oakland engine had a smaller size bore and stroke than the Viking's, was redesigned with a down-draft carburetor and was smoother and quieter than other V-8s of the day. This V-8 powered the car from 5 to 35 mph in 10.4 seconds, and enabled it to climb an 11% grade at the GM Proving Ground in five seconds less than the average car.
The 1930 Series 452 Cadillac Imperial Landaulette (far right), built by Fleetwood, was one of 33 body styles available on the limited production V-16.

60

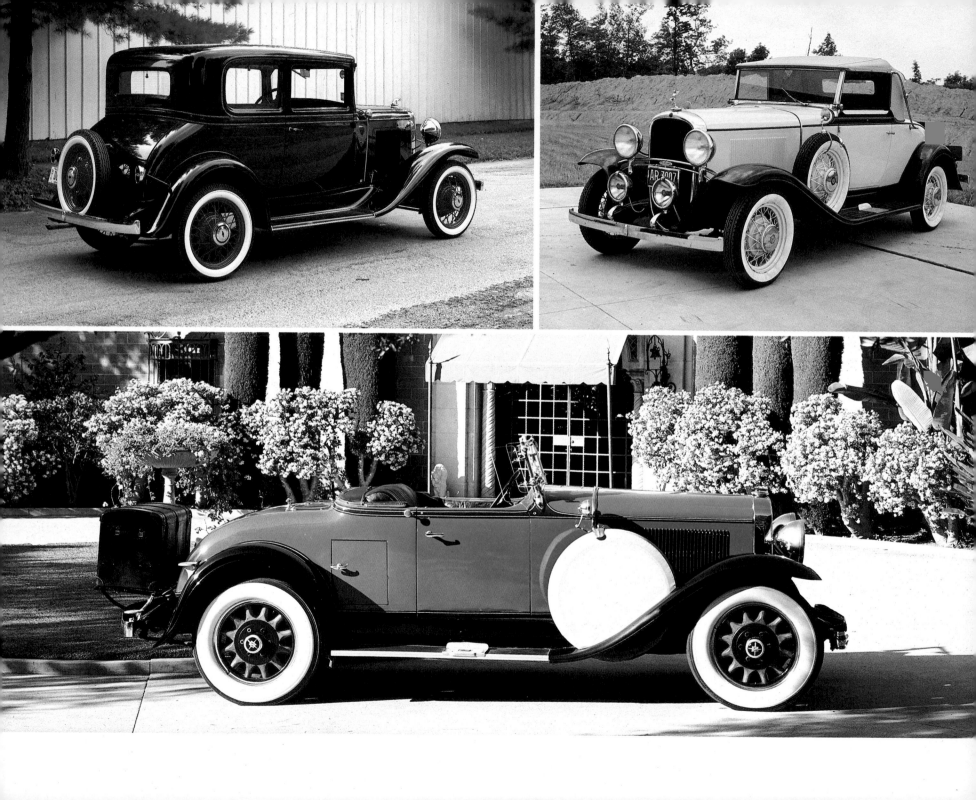

Accessories began to play an increasing part in the public's taste for add-on equipment. Independent manufacturers' quality was often as high as it was dubious. The official GM accessories would set a standard from which all were judged. Chevrolet accessories for 1931 included rear trunk rack, spotlight, cloth spare tire covers, special bumpers and clocks. (Far left top) 1931 Chevrolet Independence Series AE, a 5 passenger coupe with a rear mounted standard spare wheel. A three-spoke, hard rubber steering wheel replaced the four-spoked, wooden-rimmed one; head and tail lights were chromed for the first time.

By 1931 a new car could come off the line every 41 seconds at Oldsmobile's new 85 acre, 26 building complex in Lansing, Michigan, enabling the division to build and ship 800 cars each day. A total of 47,279 Olds were shipped for the year. (Near left top) the popular 6 cyl. Oldsmobile F-31 convertible roadster. This was the first year Oldsmobile was to offer Synchro-Mesh transmission.

The 1931 Buick Series 50 Model 54 sport roadster (left bottom) with golf compartment had a new straight eight engine with overhead valves, available in three horsepower and displacement ranges. All models used up-draft carburetors and an automatic vacuum-operated spark advance, doing away with the spark lever on the steering column. Both Cadillac and Buick introduced vaccuum-operated clutches in this year. Prior to production the new Buicks had logged hundreds of thousands of miles testing the new engines, a standard procedure at the GM Proving Ground.

Pontiacs for 1931 were longer and lower. A special feature was the extended rear quarter window with thinner rear pillar, adding higher visibility and a graceful roof line. (Right bottom) 1931 Pontiac coupe. The new Pontiac for 1931 was the Pontiac convertible (right top). Once the least expensive of the line the convertible, with new styles, more power and windup windows, moved up on the price schedule as public attitude began changing toward the open car.

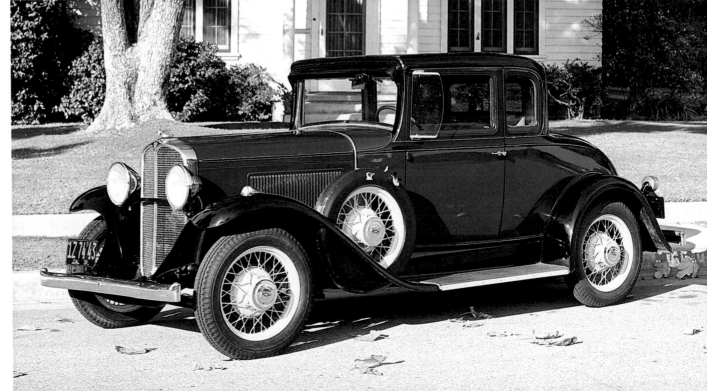

GREYHOUND

GM's longstanding relationship with Greyhound began with the Z-250, then considered to be the ultimate in long distance cross-country coaches. Introduced at the 1929 Atlantic City Show it forecast the long graceful lines reflecting the company's running mascot, the fleet greyhound.

The Type V was mechanically the same as the Z-250, and shorter by only one window. However it championed a very quick disconnect engine for easy removal. Early GM buses were powered by sleeve-valve engines suitable for big city, slow, stop-and-go traffic, but troublesome for long distance straightaways. The sleeve-valve engines were converted to poppet valve until replaced with newer engines of GM design.

The bus' shape would change in the mid 1930's from a boxy round bread loaf to a streamlined streak when the angle-drive system, invented by Dwight Austin, placed the engine sideways, tucking it in back, saving both internal and external space.

(Left) 1933 S-400, a 21 passenger streamlined bus with 400 cu. in. engine. (Above) 1931 Type V suburban coach. (Below) 1930 Z-250, with a 250 in. wheelbase it was the biggest intercity coach.

As GM entered the 1930's the Art and Colour Section was given additional responsibility for GM trucks and buses. At left are two examples of GM's "stream style," showing the cab integrated with the entire body, recessed rear fenders and fender skirts increasing the aerodynamic line. This "stream style" was made visibly present with a chrome belt line in flight from the slim vertical, louvered radiator straight to the rear curving around to the back.

The production model of the 1936 T-23B (left top), with a new set-back, wider-tread axle and a wheelbase choice of 136 to 196 in., was powered by a 257 cu. in., 87.5 hp, valve-in-head straight six. Vacuum boosted four-wheel brakes and a range of dual tone colors were available. An equally splendid example of the "stream style" was the 1936 F-61C, a variation of the cab-over-engine, or COE, (left bottom). The 7 tonner, with a set-forward axle, was powered by a 400 cu. in., 110 hp straight six. Wheelbases were available from 108 to 196 in.

The 1930's GM line covered payloads up to 15 tons on 4 and 6 wheelers. For a period of time GM built its own trailers. One of the main innovations in the late 1920's and early 1930's was the sleeper-cab option. (Near right top) 1932 T-51 GM semi-trailer tractor.

The mid 1930's would see a return of the COE for inner city service. (Far right top) 1934 GM T-75 tanker with the typical COE.

An example of one of GM's first attempts at a personalization of a large tractor trailer is the 1932 semi-trailer tractor made for J.R. Caldwell (right bottom).

In 1935 hydraulic brakes were available. Total GM truck production in 1937 surpassed 50,000. Two years later GM had perfected the 2 cycle Diesel engine, introduced throughout the GM line and destined to change the economy of the truck through the use of lower-cost Diesel fuel.

Another important contribution to trucking in the 1930's was the equipping of large trucks with GM's Frigidaire units to carry perishable freight from farm to market—a step that would change not only the agricultural economy but the table menu in millions of homes.

66

The most notable mechanical innovation in 1932 was Buick's Wizard Control, which allowed drivers to shift the Synchro-Mesh transmission from second to third without using the clutch. (Below) 1932 Buick Series 90 Model 91. (Near left) 1932 Chevrolet Confederate Series BA 7 window sedan. (Above) 1932 Cadillac Series 355-B V-8 convertible coupe. This was the first year Cadillac offered optional wheel discs. The 1932 Cadillac V-16 Madame X (far left), a resplendent 149 in. wheelbased limo, was built for R. S. McLaughlin, President of GM of Canada.

In 1932 GM, along with other manufacturers, suffered losses in sales. Many well-known automobile producers such as Stutz, Auburn, Cord, Pierce Arrow, and Duesenberg were to gradually phase out, and would be gone by the end of the 1930's. In 1933 all GM cars featured No-Draft Ventilation; one year later they featured independent front suspension, called Knee-Action. This was the last year for Buick's Series 90 5 passenger Victoria coupe (above). In this year Chevrolet began sponsorhip of the most famous of all youth events, the American Soap Box Derby. The "Blue Flame" cylinder head, developed by Chevy in 1934, generated 15 more horsepower without any increase in engine displacement, boasting "80 horsepower at 80 miles per hour." (Below) 1933 Chevrolet CA Deluxe roadster convertible. In 1933 Pontiac introduced a revised series of cars powered by a straight eight engine, known as the Economy Eight. The side valve motor of 223.4 cu. in. and 77 hp increased gas mileage more than 10%. (Right) 1933 Pontiac Economy Straight Eight sport coupe.

The 1933 Chicago World's Fair Cadillac show-car, a V-16 Fastback Coupe, is remembered as one of the great automobile designs. Its all-steel roof was imperative to the stylists' desire to shake free from the evolutionary transition concept in favor of a truly revolutionary approach. Stylists were searching for a purity of body line, to keep the form simple, uncluttered and flowing in a unified line that gracefully swept through the hood into the body, terminating in the fastback.

The trunk for the first time was built in, the spare tire hidden, making the protruding fender wells no longer necessary. The rear fenders were gently sculptured out of the smooth body to harmonize with the curving lines of the roof and the back. The individual front fenders captured the essence of the racing aircraft wheel wind fairing, balancing neatly with the mandatorily retained front end, and signified Cadillac's heritage of the period. New, too, was the belt line accented by a thin highlight of chrome to unify the strikingly new shape.

The 1934 production model Series 452-D Fleetwood fastback coupe (right) retained the V-16 engine and the major lines of the World's Fair car. Absent is the recessed license plate with light above, the gas filler built in the top of the tail light and chrome window edging.

In 1934 Buick produced an all-new car born of the first modernized plant built since 1925. The big news, as with other GM cars, was its independent Knee-Action suspension in the front and the ride stabilizer in the rear, both developed by GM engineers. The prestigious Rolls-Royce asked for and received patent rights for these technical advances for its Phantom III. New, too, for the 1934 Buick was an accelerator operated switch engaging the starter motor, safety glass windshield and side vent windows.

(Left top) 1934 Buick Phaeton Series 60 Model 68-C. (Left center) 1934 Pontiac Cabriolet 2 passenger convertible, considered one of the year's most attractive cars with a GM first, a die-cast side grille, and contrasting body and fender color scheme. (Left bottom) 1934 LaSalle Model 350 convertible coupe for export.

Two of America's prime and most lasting names in the art of coach building are Fisher Body and Fleetwood Metal Body Company, both producing bodies for the pioneer automobile companies. Fisher began in Detroit in 1908 and became a GM division in 1926. It has come to be known throughout the world for outstanding achievement in the technology of building bodies for mass production.

Fleetwood was founded at the turn of the century in Fleetwood, Pennsylvania, becoming well-known for designing special bodies for foreign as well as American automobiles. Fleetwood was acquired by Fisher in 1925 and moved to Detroit in January 1931, concentrating almost exclusively on Cadillacs and LaSalles.

A superb example of American coach work by Fleetwood is the graceful 1934 Cadillac V-16 Victoria 5 passenger convertible Model 452-D (right). Long, sleek, perfectly proportioned in every detail, with a 154 in. wheelbase that was the longest of any American luxury car, it could have been of any dimension, so perfect were its proportions. Its wire wheels are enclosed with wheel discs, a style at the time considered to be an adjunct to the "aerodynamic" line for a hundred-mile-an-hour motorcar. The Fleetwood Victoria epitomizes many of the outstanding contributions Cadillac made during the period of what is now considered the Golden Age of the Classic Automobile.

The Victoria has a split windshield—a trademark of Fleetwood-bodied Cadillacs— telescopic bumpers, teardrop fenders and rear skirts that would eventually become standard for many of GM's lines.

The V-16 engine would later be eclipsed in performance, if not beauty. For example GM's 1941 V-8, a 346 cu. in. 150 hp engine with a compression ratio of 7.25, could accelerate 0–60 in 14 seconds, with a maximum speed of 100 mph—an almost ideal and pragmatic power plant. Cadillac's V-8 would be one of those unique engines that could be refined over and over, seemingly endlessly ripe for improvement in every aspect.

LOCOMOTIVES

At the GM Science and Technology exhibit at the 1933 Century of Progress World's Fair in Chicago, one of the most dramatic exhibits was the Chevrolet assembly line powered by two experimental 600 hp, 8 cyl. Diesel engines. These engines, the result of several years of development by Charles Kettering at GM's Research Laboratories, marked the beginning of America's Diesel-powered trains. Ralph Budd, president of Burlington Railroad, challenged GM to build two Diesel engines for his streamliner. On the first test run the Burlington's Zephyr streamliner (top inset) exceeded 100 mph. Other railroads began ordering Diesels from GM's Electro-Motive Division—the beginning of the end of steam's century of dominance. Today the stainless steel Zephyr is exhibited at Chicago's Museum of Science and Industry.

The train that earned the title of "the single greatest locomotive of the 20th century" by pioneering the full conversion to Diesel power on American railroads is at far right. The 1939 GM Diesel freight train made a grueling 83,764 mi. demonstration run carrying a varying load over 20 railroad lines in 35 states, proving that the Diesel could do twice the work of steam at half the cost.

"The most famous face in all Diesel history," reported *Trains* magazine "was the high operating cab set up behind a round nose," the creation of GM stylists and engineers of the Electro-Motive Division (bottom inset). Built in the new GM La Grange, Illinois locomotive plant in 1937 and 1938 it was the first time ever that a production locomotive was to be completely designed from start, sweeping away every wind resisting obstruction, providing a low drag penetration and a more streamlined shape that has remained a beautiful unification of purpose and line. The first of this all-new series of locomotives took honors as the "world's most powerful locomotive." In the fuel conscious 1980's railroads began to reappraise the beauty of streamlining and its cost effectiveness.

The all-new 1936 Buicks, with smoothly rounded corners and enveloping fenders, were popular at home and abroad. Those exported to England were fitted with right-hand drive and British headlights. King Edward VII ordered a Buick (near right), a standard Limited Model 90-LX body with custom body work added by GM of Canada. A redesigned 320 cu. in. 8 cyl. engine, developing 120 hp and featuring aluminum "Anolite" pistons with shaped domes, powered most Buicks that year. The Cabriolet convertible (below) was Chevy's only open car in 1936, its Silver Anniversary year. The lightest, possibly the fastest, Pontiac Eight of 1935 was the Pontiac Improved Eight Business Coupe (far right), a 2 passenger.

In 1936 Chevrolet celebrated its 25th Anniversary. During the 1930's the division's dealers averaged, for seven years straight, sales of one million per year and over 11 million trade-ins. The anniversary Chevy featured an all-steel body, "Box Girder" frame, 16 in. wheels and a hydraulic brake system exclusive to Chevy. The brake system gave superior stopping power and enabled the division to advertise the "safest car money can buy."
(Left) 1936 ½ ton pickup. (Right) 1935 Master Deluxe Sport Coupe. (Below) 1936 Town Sedan Model FC.

GM'S PARADE OF PROGRESS

The most popular exhibit of the 1933 Chicago World's Fair was GM's Science and Technology display, which presented to the Depression-wearied audiences a glimpse of reassurance of progress and a bright look into the future. The display sparked the idea of a traveling show to reach those who could not attend the Chicago World's Fair.

The first of three Parades of Progress opened on February 11, 1936 in Lakeland, Florida and was brought to town by a caravan of eight huge red and white vans. Custom built by Fisher Body's Fleetwood plant, each streamliner (right) spanned a 223 in. wheelbase truck chassis and was powered by a GMC gasoline engine.

Canvas awnings joined six of the vans to form walk-through exhibits. Nine GMC and Chevrolet tractor trailers were also employed to haul the Parade's equipment and additional exhibits, and a 1936 Chevy "command car" acted as a mobile office.

All five of GM's automobile divisions were represented by models that were traded in at local dealers every 2000 miles of the route. Playing mostly in the country's small towns the Parade moved with the seasons, even traveling to Mexico in January 1938. GM used the entertaining and educational free road show to communicate its message to the public; there were no "sales gimmicks" behind the dioramas and exhibits. Some of the "marvels" shown to audiences were a pingpong game in stereophonic sound, a microwave oven that fried an egg but did not burn a newspaper and a sound that traveled on a flashlight beam. Even Oldsmobile's "Old Scout" was restored to travel with the Parade, being cranked up at every showing. Its purpose was to point out the differences among the early cars and those of the 1930's.

In 1940 the original vans were replaced by a dozen new ones called Futurliners. Each van (left) featured special power steering to turn the twin wheels. By the time of Pearl Harbor, which canceled the second Parade, the exhibit had traveled over a million miles to 251 towns in the U.S., Canada, Mexico and Cuba, and was viewed by 12.5 million people. The postwar Parade was reactivated in 1953, but three years later it was replaced by the future it foretold, the television, which offered free shows right in people's living rooms.

After spending $26 million in tooling Chevrolet celebrated the debut of its 1937 models on November 7, 1936 with 50,000 employees the guests at several thousand "Chevrolet breakfasts" from coast to coast.

Everything about the 1937 Chevrolet seemed new and everything seemed right. It was extraordinarily well received. This year's Chevy, with the previous year's hydraulic brake system, Knee-Action ride and all-steel body, was given a new 216.5 cu. in., 85 hp, 6 cyl. engine—a compact improved "Cast Iron Wonder" that was more wonderful than ever. The new frame, which added 4 in. to overall body width, and the new hypoid axle, which lowered the floor some 2 in., created more interior space and an opportunity to create a well executed exterior that made this year's Chevrolet an important transition model, continuing it as the number one sales leader. The 1937 Master Coupe (left top) offered an optional "coupe delivery," and the shift lever was transferred to the steering column.

As the nation's economy picked up automobile sales began to once again reach record-breaking heights. By 1937 all GM cars featured all-steel body construction.

Oldsmobile, completely restyled in 1937 with a greater difference emphasized between the 6 and 8 cyl., introduced a safety 4 speed transmission with the shift lever transferred to the steering column as an option of the 8's—the first step to Olds' exclusive Hydra-matic introduced three years later. As on other 1937 GM cars front and rear stabilizers were standard; windshield defrosters were optional. Olds topped its 1936 slogan "The Cars That Have Everything" with a record-breaking 212,767 cars built in 1937, adding up to the division's best sales year to date—clearly indicating that the Depression had more than waned. (Left bottom) the most popular Olds, the 2 door Model F-37.

The 1937 Pontiac convertible sedan (right top) featured a weather-proof folding top that lowered into a compartment behind the rear seat and removable center pillars.

The 1937 LaSalle, with major restyling, a longer wheelbase of 124 in. and a return to the V-8 engine, would record its biggest sales year in history. This year would see the last of the Cadillac V-12 engines. (Right bottom) LaSalle Series 50 business coupe.

Buick styling reached a highpoint in 1938, though the most important changes were mechanical. Engineering developments included a new Dynaflash engine with high compression domed pistons, improved combustion chambers, torque free springing, an all-coil front and rear spring suspension, a long-sought "self shift" semi-automatic transmission (shared with Oldsmobile) and new frames and weight reductions. Also for the first time this year a car radio was optional. (Far left) 1938 Buick Special Sport Coupe Model 46-C. Buick continued to be a favorite with foreign coach builders; including Letourneur et Marchand, who added coach work to the 1938 Buick Special Model 46-C (near left). (Above) 1937 Buick Model 48 Special sedan. (Below) 1938 Chevrolet Master Deluxe in police trim.

Harley Earl's Buick Y-Job of 1938 (above and below) created an all-new way of looking at the shape of the automobile by eliminating the car's center cube with its flat vertical reach from runningboard to roof by first lowering the body to achieve a horizontal line, eliminate the running boards, softly round all lines and roll under the body panels. All sections of the car were unified, beginning at the front, where for the first time the grille was horizontal and symmetrically balanced with bumper. Also for the first time fenders softly curved around and flowed into the side door. Front fender shapes were repeated in the back fenders gently tapering to parallel the rear deck. Almost unneeded were the chrome strips visually uniting the fenders. The Y-Job would preface a generation of dream cars and anticipate the styling of the 1940's. Built on a standard 1938 Buick chassis it included other innovations: power windows, power top, power door locks and power steering. The 1938 Cadillac 60 Special (right) was a styling milestone marking the beginning of a new, smaller Cadillac. Lower than any previous Cadillac it spurned styling clichés, running boards and excessive chrome trim; it uniquely featured convertible-type window frames. It was the first mass produced car to have distinct upper and lower halves. The trunk was an integral part of the car's design; its notchback styling would inspire automotive design well into the 1950's.

In 1935 Opel launched its smallest and least expensive car of all, the P-4 (below). Substantial numbers were built without change from 1935 through 1938. At the Berlin Show in 1937, Opel's 75th anniversary year, the magnificent Admiral was unveiled. Its 75 bhp engine, powering the car to a top speed of 80 mph, and its 3 speed transmission closely resembled those of the contemporary Chevrolet. (Far right top) 1938 Admiral convertible. (Far right center) 1938 Admiral sedan. The 1938 Opel Kadett (near right) utilizing 4 cyl., 1.1 liter, 23 hp engine, was an exceptionally popular car, with some 107,000 units being produced before World War II. A new 6 cyl. engine was installed in a Kapitän in November 1938, when the first models appeared. The well-styled Kapitän offered a unitized body frame, parallel-wishbone front suspension with coil springs and a torsion anti-roll bar that was very advanced for that time. (Far right bottom) 1939 Kapitän.

OPEL EXPANDS

During the first year of the GM-Opel merger relatively few changes were made in the German marque's cars, though a new range was planned for 1931—the same year the new Opel Blitz trucks were announced. At a 1930 meeting in Frankfurt, where the handsome new Opels were unveiled, Alfred P. Sloan Jr., President of GM, voiced his anticipation that Opel's annual production—then at 26,000 plus units—might one day reach 150,000 vehicles. Though Sloan's statement met with derision at the time, only eight years later Opel's annual production of 140,500 vehicles came within 94% of that seemingly unattainable figure.

Opel's big news at the 1935 Berlin show was the Olympia, which was the first quantity-built German car with an integral steel frame and body, and also the first car in the world of its size and price class with this weight-saving construction.

Strict regulations, begun in 1934, banned the exportation of currency from Germany. By June 1940 GM resigned all responsibilities for Opel activities. When Opel production was stopped on October 1940 production totalled 1,003,585 units, a great achievement for Opel and the entire German motorcar industry.

After the war, with its factory in rubble, Opel was forced to start from scratch. Production of Opel parts began in May 1945, the same year the Soviet Union removed the Kadett's tooling. One year later the Moskvitch 400, a pre-war Kadett look-alike until 1959, made its debut in Russia.

As Opel struggled to return to truck and car production GM debated whether to resume control of the unpromising operation. An affirmative decision was officially made on November 1, 1948.

The year 1939 was one of transition at GM, as most cars were being prepared for the modernity of the 1940's. For Buick 1939 marked the beginning of the subtle blending of chrome and grilles into the new flowing body lines, a departure from surface-mounting. (Above) 1939 Buick 46-C Sport Convertible. (Near right) 1939 Buick 48 Special with a sunroof offered for the first time on this marque, an option first offered on Cadillacs in 1938 and made available on all marques except Chevrolet in 1939. The year 1939 was the first one in which turn signals started to become standard on GM models. (Below) 1939 Chevrolet Master Deluxe 4 door sedan, Series JA. (Far right top) 1939 Pontiac Deluxe 8 Sport Coupe. Pontiac would introduce an all-new eight for the next year. (Far right bottom) 1939 Chevrolet ½ ton pickup, Series JC.

93

Greyhound Lines

OWNER AND OPERATOR
ATLANTIC GREYHOUND CORPORATION
CHARLESTON, WEST VIRGINIA

EXPRESS 1

2001

The 1939 "Silversides" (left) was a trademark vehicle made exclusively by GM for Greyhound. Introduced in 1939 at the New York World's Fair as an updated version of the "Cruiser," it featured a 2 cycle, 6 cyl., in-line, transversely mounted Diesel engine and GM Frigidaire air conditioning. This series continued until the early 1950's.

Between 1936 and 1938 GM introduced the double decker transit bus, dubbed the "Queen Mary" (right top). The 72 passenger Model 720 featured a low floor, a wide front entrance door, a Dwight angle-drive system and a Banker automatic transmission. Built for the transit systems of New York and Chicago, it was used as late as 1953 in New York City.

The 1936 Greyhound Cruiser (right center), an intercity coach, was a revolution in transportation. The Cruiser featured a body of monocoque construction, a rear engine and a luggage compartment between the axles and passenger seats. The safe, weatherproof luggage compartment area, reachable from either side, was utilized for intercity as well as long distance package shipping. Greyhound provided a network of shipping and receiving stations. The Cruiser's superb styling was the Art and Colour Section's first major involvement in coach design.

In 1934 Greyhound completed extensive tests of three coach prototypes. GM was to build 1462 models exclusively for Greyhound between the years 1936 and 1939.

The 1938 Model 740 transit bus (right bottom) began a famous GM power team—a transverse, 2 cycle, 6 cyl. GM Diesel and Hydraulic Drive. Air conditioning was introduced in buses in 1938.

The replacement of trolleys by buses in the 1930's was a gradual evolution attributed to many factors, the most visible being the mobility and versatility of the bus as opposed to the rigidity of the trolley system.

95

CHAPTER FIVE
THE WAR INTERRUPTS
1940-1949

With the dawn of the 1940's a new sense of urgency pervaded the nation as it pulled itself out of the Depression. The changes that took place at GM were an energetic response to the worst economic times and the most perilous political situation the world had yet known. The year 1940 was a pivotal one introducing the torpedo-type body style, bold grilles, heavier bumpers and the blending of headlights into the fenders.

The eleven-year reign of the legendary V-16 engine would end, as would the era of the LaSalle, which had established automotive styling as a major factor in mass production and distribution. It was a year offering the promise of prosperity. On January 11, 1940 at 11 AM GM produced its twenty-five-millionth car, appropriately a Chevrolet painted silver.

The thoroughly modern automobiles to come from GM would be direct descendants of Harley Earl's Buick Y-Job and William L. Mitchell's, Earl's successor as head of the GM Styling staff, prototype of the Cadillac 60 Special. One of the most admired and pace-setting creations in automotive history the 60 Special had been placed in production in 1938.

The new car had a double-dropped frame, large kickup over the rear axle and sturdy cross members in combination with siderails of reduced depth that allowed for a greatly reduced floor level. The well-balanced body, expansive areas of glass and subtle touches of bright metal, resulted in a platform for some of the most beautiful Cadillac models ever built and initiated styling changes throughout GM's product lines. The time-honored V-8, redesigned and refined, would become the dominant power plant in peace and war.

Early in 1940 Chevrolet was awarded the first U.S. Government contract for war materials—75 mm high-

explosive shells. Military trucks, anti-aircraft gun parts, shells and aircraft engines became part of Pontiac's output. Shortly thereafter the speed of GM's transformation to wartime production increased tremendously, the bulk of the change occurring within a few months of 1942. Until 1941 hope held forth against the inevitable war, and factories continued to hum the notes of economic well-being.

In 1941 Fleetwood made the incomparably beautiful Cadillac 60 Special and the stately 75 Series limousine. Such independent coach builders as Brunn, Bohman and Swartz and Coachcraft were keenly attracted to the new Cadillac's all-modern chassis and the most powerful, quietest running engine available.

The 250,117 Buicks produced by May 28, 1940 exceeded by one car the division's greatest model year production since 1928; on the average, 100 Buicks were sold a day. The 1940 Buick received the torpedo body style for its Super and Roadmaster series. The following year the new fastback sedans and coupes completed the line of bodies with the Special and Century. Buicks utilizing the "Fireball 8" 165 hp straight engine were the highest-powered standard production automobiles built in America.

In 1941 316,251 Buick automobiles were produced at a clip of 76 units per hour for an enthusiastic public that was quickly adjusting to the economic turnaround. The two-millionth Oldsmobile was also produced that year. Chevrolet continued to top the market with 1,250,281 cars and trucks produced. On the day that would live in infamy, December 7, 1941, the nation was shocked into war by the attack on Pearl Harbor. Between February 10, 1942 and September 9, 1945 not a single passenger car for civilian use would leave a GM assembly line. All of GM would be dedicated to the nation's war effort.

The convertible has always had the fascination of a new romance and has been as unpredictable. The open car, irrespective of adventuresome ads, was always launched in trepidation. By hindsight it is the most remembered automobile, the highest priced collectible. The 1940's saw an increase in the convertible's popularity. Chevrolet's most expensive car in 1940 was the Special DeLuxe Convertible (above). Buick's elegant 1940 Limited Model 80-C Phaeton convertible (below) was outsold by the rebirth of the station wagon super line Series 50. Convertibles would wax and wane in popularity and by the late 1970's would sputter out. The last GM-built convertible would be the 1976 Cadillac Eldorado. As could be expected but not predicted with precision the convertible would rise again in the 1980's.

Pontiac's see-through World's Fair and Golden Gate showcar of 1940 (right) was based on the DeLuxe Six 4 door touring sedan.

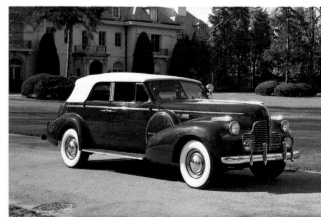

The notchback styling of the Cadillac 60 Special directly influenced the 1940 Oldsmobile, Buick, Pontiac and LaSalle. (Left) a brace of Pontiac Torpedo Eights with Pontiac's own highly "streamlined, ultra modern" version of Silver Streak styling. In 1941 Pontiac went Torpedo all the way offering interchanging 6 and 8 cyl. engines for 11 various body styles. Sales soared to a new record high—buyers having seen the torpedo style rushed to the showrooms—283,601 Pontiacs for 1941, with 16,685 1942 models off the line before Pearl Harbor.

Oldsmobile also had a great thing going for it—probably one of the most significant and important advances in automobile history—the Hydra-matic Drive. First introduced on the 1940 models the fully automatic transmission cost $57.00 less than the safety automatic transmission it replaced. The top-of-the-line 1940 Oldsmobile Series 90 (above) offered two-tone factory paint as an option.

Both GMC and Chevrolet built a 2 door, 6–7 passenger station wagon powered by a 228 cu. in., 87 hp, straight six engine. The chassis of the GMC wagon, called the Suburban, was interchangeable with that of the Chevrolet Carryall. (Below) 1941 GMC version of the station wagon.

Some of Cadillac's most important engineering developments as well as its most beautiful cars made their debut in the early 1940's. The spectacular Series 62, which offered four streamlined Fisher torpedo body styles on a new 129 in. wheelbase, were the most stylish of all 1940 Cadillacs. With a wider, lower and more integrated look, the Series 62 cars clearly reflected the 60 Special's styling influence. They featured a 45° angle windshield, curved rear windows and concealed door hinges. (Left top) 1940 Cadillac Series 62 convertible. All 1940 V-8 Cadillacs, including the Series 62, sported new massive die-cast grilles. The corporation was no longer cautious about putting chrome on the front ends of its models.

"Sealed Beam" headlamps, introduced in 1940, were the result of a joint effort among the automotive industry, lamp manufacturers and other interested groups. A commendable contribution to driving safety the headlamps consisted of a sealed unit that maintained its efficiency throughout the lamp's life. Cadillacs and LaSalles, like most 1940 American cars, were equipped with this new feature. Parking lights incorporating new standard turn indicators were now mounted on the Cadillac's front fenders. Running boards, a fading feature, were still optional on 1940 Cadillacs and LaSalles.

After a 14 year model run the last LaSalle, a 4 door torpedo-styled sedan, left the factory on August 26, 1940. A total of 10,380 LaSalles were sold that year. (Left bottom) 1940 Series 52 LaSalle Club Coupe with a smooth, uncluttered torpedo body shape.

The Cadillac V-16, after 11 years of production, also ended in 1940. The dazzling Cadillac V-16 models were significant factors in elevating the division's leadership in the luxury car market. The eggcrate grille of 1934 to 1940 was specific to the V-16 model as illustrated on a 1940 Series 90 Fleetwood (right). With a 101 in. wheelbase the Series 90 was available in a convertible and a touring sedan with and without a divider window, a trunk-back convertible sedan, formal sedans for both 5 and 7 passengers and a variety of 7 passenger sedans.

In 1941 Buick offered the greatest variety of models in its history—26 separate body styles available in five distinct series. The division also enjoyed its greatest production year to date—316,215 cars during the 1941 calendar year. Styling of the 1941 Buicks was quite different from the 1940 models; the front license plate bracket was, for the first time, designed as an integral part of the bumper. Also, as on other GM cars that year, headlamps were now blended into the front fenders rather than bolted in separate stampings, and front fenders on all series ran back to the front doors to smoothly blend into the shape of the body and rocker panels. Gone forever from all Buicks were exposed running boards and fender-mounted sidemounts. However the major change in the 1941 Buicks was in power, rather than styling.

In 1941 the "Fireball 8" engine was introduced, featuring a new fuel system called "Compound Carburetion" and delivering 125 hp in the Special and Super Series and 165 hp in the Century, Roadmaster and Limited Series. (Left top) 1941 Buick Century Sedanet Model 66-S.

Totally new in the Buick Special line was the beautifully styled 1941 Estate Wagon Model 49 (right) which sported an all-wood body. The station wagon was destined to become one of the most popular body types in America.

Fastback styling dominated the 1941 model year, although Chevrolet did not introduce its fastback model until the following year. In 1941 Chevy moved toward larger cars with a 116 in. wheelbase, 3 in. longer than the 1940 models. The new Chevy bodies no longer featured running boards, although a vestige remained on the doors, a slight flair covering a concealed "safety-step." Also gone this year were the hood side panels, as the hood now opened from the front—a feature first seen in 1940 models. The engines of this year's Chevys had a power increase to 90 hp.

The 1941 Chevrolet Special Deluxe Fleetline 4 door sedan (left center) was introduced at mid-year and attracted a surprising number of buyers for a short-run style. The car, which was considered a one-model subseries of the Special Deluxe Series, featured a newly designed roof and upper body without rear quarter windows.

In 1941 Oldsmobile built its two-millionth car and reached an all-time high in calendar year sales—270,040 units. This year, for the first time, Oldsmobile offered three lines of cars on two wheelbases, with a 6 and 8 cyl. engine interchangeable in all three lines. (Left bottom) 1941 Oldsmobile 98 Club Coupe with 125 in. wheelbase.

The 1941 year-end sales figures registered records for Pontiac and Cadillac. In 1941 Pontiac became the largest producer in its price class with sales of 330,061 cars. (Below) the 1941 V-8 Torpedo Sedan Coupe. (Far left top) 1941 Torpedo Custom Sedan. Pontiac models offered 8 cyl. engines on two chassis of 119 and 122 in., respectively.

Cadillac sold a record 66,130 cars in 1941 and further established its fine styling reputation. Headlights were now integrated into the new wide front fenders, while parking and turn signal lamps were incorporated into the grille's upper outer edges. Hydra-matic automatic transmission, power-operated convertible top, automatic heating system and air conditioning were also offered in Cadillacs. The 1941 Series 62 convertible (far left bottom) marked the end of Cadillac's 4 door soft top sedan. The 1941 4 door 60 Special sedan (near left) gave a hint of the 1942 styling with front fender shell extending into the door.

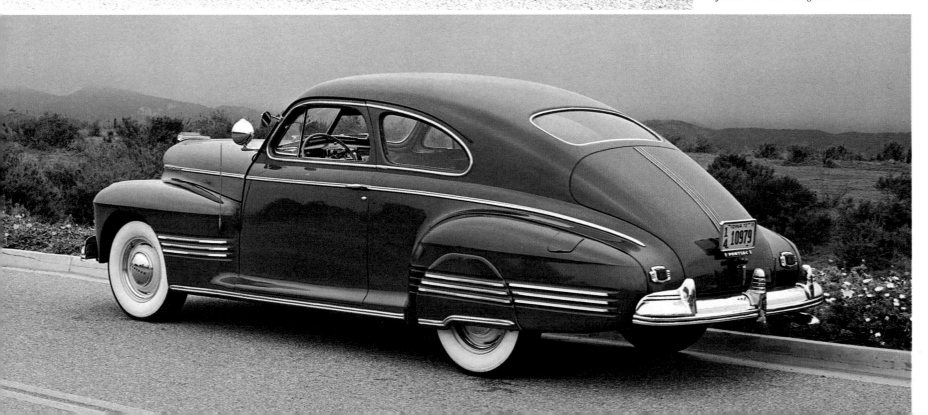

With World War II now a reality for America the country began to channel all its resources toward military production. However since 1942 model production began in the fall of 1941, manufacturers were able to produce a number of 1942 cars before the government halted all nonessential civilian production.

Despite the dwindling supply of materials, Buick managed to give its cars a new look. A major styling innovation was the "Airfoil" fender, a swept-back fender styling first tried on a special Cadillac, called "The Duchess," that was built for the Duke of Windsor. The 1942 Buick Super Model 56-C convertible (above) sported the new "Airfoil" fenders, as did the Buick Roadmaster Series. These models marked the first time a major American car had front fenders sweeping the body's length until they met the leading edges of the rear fenders.

One of the most perfectly styled Chevrolets to date was the 1941 Special Deluxe Club Coupe (right). The 5 passenger model, a favorite of the young set, featured a convertible top that folded back when the driver operated a valve that controlled a vacuum-power linkage. It had a production run of 155,889 units.

After January 1, 1942 the government prohibited the use of chrome trim, hence, all trim pieces were patiently hand painted in harmonizing colors for the remainder of the 1942 calendar year. Known as "blackout models" these chromeless cars were officially halted on February 2, 1942. With the end of GM's civilian production in early 1942—Chevrolet on January 30, Buick on February 2, Cadillac on February 4, Oldsmobile on February 5 and Pontiac on February 10— 27½ million passenger cars were registered in the U.S., a number that was reduced by five million by 1944. For starting in February 1942 GM, like the rest of the automotive industry, would turn to military production.

WORLD WAR II

GM's contribution to the winning of the war in Europe and the Pacific was one of its greatest challenges as well as one of its greatest achievements. In this brief space one can but fleetingly touch upon this unequalled accomplishment. The success of GM's tremendous wartime role lay in the genius of its peacetime managerial philosophy. Decentralized, highly flexible, local responsibility made possible the almost overnight conversion by its 36 divisions to building and supplying a war machine. It was a war machine of such magnitude that it enabled the American and allied fighting men and women to successfully conduct an all-out global war.

The magnitude of GM's challenge rested with the administrative units of local management providing individual initiative to carry out the herculean task of converting peacetime production to war in the shortest time possible—a timetable of days and months never believed possible by the enemy. GM entered into war production with an invaluable asset to the nation of having long experience of working with thousands of other manufacturers skilled in the supply of specialized items. Over 20,000 outside suppliers and subcontractors would mesh with 94 GM plants in 46 communities over 13 states, not to mention Canada, Mexico, South America and the wholly owned companies, subsidiaries and partnership plants of the allied nations. This vast network, unmatched by any other manufacturer or industrial nation, would produce a range of material, services, and training of civilian and military personnel that is beyond the possibility of recording here.

To facilitate the service and maintenance of its war products GM supplied a staff of its own technicians on fighting fronts and established GM-operated training schools in the U.S. which, at the conclusion of the war, trained 62,346 Army and Navy instructors and technicians, providing the nucleus of trained mechanics for servicing GM-built war equipment.

GM's contribution spanned virtually every conceivable product. The division produced military supplies from the tiniest ball bearing, watch-like precision instruments, to massive tanks, naval ships, fighting planes, bombers, guns, cannons and projectiles. Rare was the military machine on land, sea or air that did not bear the stamp of GM. The list is staggering, easily filling every page of this present book and more.

A sampling of GM's war production firepower included the 20 and 37 mm aircraft guns, Oerlikon and Bofors anti-aircraft cannons, 76 mm tank and anti-tank cannons, components and gun mounts for naval 3 and 5 in. guns, volume production of .45 cal. sub-machine guns, .30 cal. carbine shells, cartridge cases, and armor piercing projectiles. GM turned out 13,000 airplanes and one-quarter of all U.S. aircraft engines.

(Far left corner top) GM Allison Division's liquid air-cooled engine powered Lockheed's P-38. Other aircraft powered by GM engines included Bell's Aircobra, Curtis War Hawk, P-51 Mustang and Grumann's Wildcat and Avenger torpedo bombers. GM produced Pratt and Whitney engines for the B-24s. Engines for larger aircraft included the Invader A-36 attack bomber, Consolidated's B-24 Liberator and numerous cargo and transport planes.

GM developed, tooled and completely built from start, in converted assembly plants during the plants' first year, 1000 Avengers and 1000 Wildcats for the Navy's carrier forces. The most intricate assignment was the aerial torpedo, requiring 5000 parts and 20,000 separate operations. Oldsmobile produced 48 million rounds of artillery ammunition, and 350,000 precision parts for aircraft engines.

GM delivered 854,000 trucks, two-thirds of all heavy-duty trucks produced. The 4 and 6 wheel drive trucks (near left bottom) were the mainstay of troop transport, mobile repair shops, airplane tenders, ambulances and the ubiquitous field kitchen.

(Far left top) Cadillac's M-5 light tank. (Far left center) Vauxhall's Churchill tank. Other armored vehicles were also an important segment of GM's war production including: M-10 Tank Destroyer and M-8 Howitzer Motor Carriage. Buick produced the T-70 Hellcat Tank Destroyer and 1000 airplane engines a month.

GM's amphibian "Duck" (far left bottom), a watertight steel hull enclosing a GM 6 wheel, 2½ ton truck was adaptable to land or to water. It was designed, tested, built and off the line in 90 days.

(Near left top) a Navy destroyer escort, one of many Navy ships powered by Cleveland Diesel Division's engines.

The war's end brought to America passion-
ate desire for peace for all nations. GM
faced a new and reverse challenge for an
all-out return to the rebuilding of America
and many of the nations of the world torn
asunder by war.

Oldsmobile got a jump on building
postwar cars in early 1945 with handbuilt
models of its 1946 cars. These were the first
such postwar cars built by any GM division
and were displayed in Lansing and major
U.S. cities as early as July 1945.
Chevrolet's first postwar model rolled off
the production line on October 3, 1945. On
October 15, 1945 the first mass-produced
postwar Oldsmobile came off the assembly
line, followed by the first postwar Cadillac
on October 17. Due to material shortages
the first Cadillacs used wooden bumpers.
The 1946 Oldsmobile 66 convertible (far left
top), with a 119 in. wheelbase, was a
resurrection of the 1942 standard GM
convertible with roll-up quarter window.
The 1947 Chevrolet Sedan delivery panel
truck (near left top), built on a car chassis,
was an ideal cross between a station wagon
and a truck designed to overcome suburban
laws prohibiting truck delivery.
(Left bottom) 1947 Pontiac Fastback, a 2
door 5 passenger coupe. In this year Silver
Streak styling was still the key to the
Pontiac design motif. Five bands of chrome
swept over the hood and down the trunk of
most models. The dramatic prewar lines of
the Torpedo Sedan Coupe accounted for a
great deal of the car's popularity. All
models carried Silver Streak deck lid molding and used rectangular shaped taillights.
In 1948 the Chevy "bowtie" emblem was
mounted on chrome-plated wings, as shown
on the 1948 Chevrolet Fleetmaster coupe
(right top). The 1948 Chevrolet Fleetmaster
station wagon (right bottom) reveals the
changed grille with a central vertical grille
bar rising to the base of the top horizontal
molding. As steel supplies began to match
their orders Chevrolet increased its production, delivering 715,992 of its 1948 models.

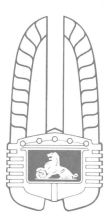

GM-HOLDEN'S

In the 1920's Holden Motor Body Builders Ltd., then one of the largest industrial enterprises in Australia, contracted with GM to use its new Woodville plant for the exclusive manufacture of GM bodies. The fruits of this agreement were rapid and profound. In 1926 General Motors (Australia) Pty. Ltd. was registered and plans were made for the sale and distribution of vehicles. It soon became obvious that a merger would mutually benefit both parties, and in 1931, GM and Holden Motor Body Builders Ltd. became General Motors-Holden's Ltd. The cornerstone had been laid for the great program of industrial expansion which was to come.

With the outbreak of World War II GMH placed its plants, personnel and all its facilities unreservedly at the disposal of the Commonwealth Government. Considering Australia's geographical isolation, relatively small population of 7½ million people and the lack of secondary supporting industries at the outbreak of the war, its subsequent industrial performance has been rightly regarded as phenomenal. A large variety of war-time products, virtually an unprecedented achievement for one company, included three different engines—aerial, naval, torpedo—a marine Diesel, four different guns, major airframe assemblies for six types of aircraft, eight types of small marine vehicles, four types of shell and bomb cases and a large number of products for the military, including over 200 bodies for military vehicles. GMH had truly come of age as a volume manufacturing unit.

World War II brought home the fact that Australia was severely handicapped because it was not able to provide its own motor transport vehicles, and the necessity to develop a strong range of secondary industries was realized. A Secondary Industries Commission was established and developed a government policy, throwing down a challenge to encourage the local manufacture of motor vehicles. GMH accepted this challenge to build an all-Australian motorcar and did so without any request for subsidy, tariff protection, import restrictions or other advantages. This decision meant the launching of one of the most significant and most complex designs for manufacturing products in industrial history and the answers had to be found in the complex economical and physical situation peculiar to Australia.

Three car prototypes were built and an 86 mi. long test track was constructed. It took 79,129 miles of testing for a fifth prototype to be deemed suitable for the varied Australian conditions.

GM assisted Australian suppliers and provided technical advice and assistance including the full use of GM laboratories, testing equipment and engineering department, enabling suppliers to initiate many new steps in manufacturing techniques to increase quality and volume.

(Left) 1948 48/215, Holden's first automobile. (Above) 1953 Holden FJ. (Right) a partial lineup of Holden automobiles in celebration of the marque's 25th Anniversary.

GMH gave birth to the first Australian designed and produced motorcar. It was indeed fitting that the then Prime Minister of Australia, the late Right Honorable J. B. Chifley, formally introduced the first Australian car to the nation and proclaimed the name selected for it on November 29, 1948. This new Australian automobile, called the 48/215, had taken four years of planning and three years to design, build and test.

By 1950 20,000 Holden cars had been produced. One reason for GMH's popularity over the years is that, alone among the cars on Australia's roads, the Holden is designed specifically for that country's conditions.

The car most associated with the Holden image was the FJ, which first came off the assembly line in October 1953; unlike its predecessor it was made available in three different models—Standard, Business and Special Sedan—with a larger engine.

In May 1953 100,000 Holdens had been built. Since that time all Holdens have been completely designed in Australia, reflecting well upon the success of the joint enterprise between the two nations.

New Zealand, because of its close association with Australia, was naturally the first choice of an export market, and in November 1954 the first consignment of assembled Holdens was exported to New Zealand. Received enthusiastically the shipment soon reached a rate of 100 per month. Today 4/5 of all Holdens marketed to New Zealand are assembled in New Zealand, further strengthening its economy and industry.

In 1957 distributorships for the Holden were established in 19 countries. Cars were exported to Hawaii, the West Indies and to an imposing total of 69 export territories. Holdens are now assembled in New Zealand, South Africa, Indonesia, Trinidad, Pakistan and the Philippines.

Holden's emblem underwent a series of changes. After its original automobile symbol, a winged man holding a miniature car and flanked by a factory, was found to be too complex for embossing, the sales and design staff submitted an Egyptian-style Wembley lion during the late 1920's. This not only catered to the then current passion for all things Egyptian, but also recalled the myth that the idea of the wheel came to primitive man while watching a lion rolling a round stone.

The famous blue and silver 1947 Train of Tomorrow (below) was the total concept of GM's Styling Section. Built by the Electro-Motive Division the patented train was offered freely to the railroads. For 2½ years it toured the U.S. and Canada, capturing the public's imagination as well as making important contributions to the railroad industry.

The 1948 Greyhound Scenicruiser prototype (left), with its famed Vista Dome, was inspired by the Train of Tomorrow, a design that was also adapted to Oldsmobile and Buick station wagons.

The 1948 GMC FC-304 medium-duty truck (near right) and 1948 GMC FF-351 medium-duty COE truck (far right), a variation of the standard cab, were typical of GM's tradition of a well established family signature for commercial vehicles.

Big news for Buick in 1948 was Dynaflow automatic drive. Offered as an option on the Roadmaster Series, public demand for the new torque converter type of transmission increased so that production facilities were first doubled, then tripled and finally quadrupled to meet orders. Within two years 85% of all Buicks would feature Dynaflow. The style leader of the 1949 Buick was the Riviera, the first mass produced hardtop with a convertible look that was shared that year with Cadillac's Coupe de Ville and Olds' Holiday Coupe. (Left) the Riviera of that year with the first sweep spear side trim and portholes that became distinctive trademarks on Buick through 1957.

On November 25, 1949 Cadillac produced its one-millionth car, a Coupe de Ville hardtop, which was the last Cadillac built during the 1940's. Cadillac's booming sales of 92,554 set a new all-time record for the division. Cadillac's most distinctive sedan was still the elegant Fleetwood 60 Special (above) with an all-new, overhead valve, V-8 engine. This engine had an important effect on the rest of the industry—the high-speed cruise, rocket acceleration and serviceability of the Oldsmobile Rocket V-8. (Below) 1949 Cadillac 62 Sedanet Club Coupe.

CHAPTER SIX

STYLING SETS THE PACE

1950-1959

The cars of the 1950's were all-new, their styling capturing the pent-up wartime desire for change with an exciting spirit bordering on the flamboyant. While the bodies were refreshingly new and modern so, too, were the engines, fulfilling the public's demand for performance. The decade saw a renewed interest in automotive sport and the rise of amateur competitors, eager to pit their skills and their cars against the competition on such courses as Watkins Glen, Elkhart Lake and Laguna Seca. These years were also the heyday of sports car clubs and the beginning of serious interest in collecting and restoring automobiles. For a public hungry for automotive news there sprang up a number of enthusiast publications.

For GM the 1950's were a series of celebrations, sales records, anniversaries and innovations in styling and engineering. The decade began with Chevrolet's introduction of Powerglide, the first automatic transmission in the low-priced field. Curved one-piece windshields, which eventually led to panoramic wraparound windshields, also first appeared in 1950. Cadillac celebrated its 50th anniversary in 1952, and along with Buick and Oldsmobile, offered power steering for the first time. In 1953 Buick celebrated the building of its seven-millionth car. GM built its fifty-millionth automobile, a 1955 Chevrolet Bel Air, in 1954. In 1956 GM of Canada produced its three-millionth car, and Adam Opel A.G. produced its two-millionth car.

GM celebrated its 50th anniversary in 1958 with a year-long Golden Milestone celebration. Cadillac built its two-millionth car the same year; it had taken 47 years to produce the first million, but just eight years to produce the second.

Intense styling competition, with a radical departure from the mainstream of evolutionary design, pervaded the industry during this decade. The 1950's were years of exciting, flamboyant two-tones, fins and high compression V-8 engines. In contrast with this postwar exuberance would be the highly functional designs of the 1960's. The first of the new group would be the smart Chevrolet Corvair of 1960. It had an all-new, air-cooled, rear-mounted aluminum block engine.

The 1950's also saw a new interest in science and advanced technology. One area of GM's pioneering research was the gas turbine engine. In addition to the Turbocruiser, the first gas turbine bus built in 1953, GM developed a series of three gas turbine Firebirds. Though not intended for production these cars were rolling test-beds for turbine application. They, along with other new developments at GM, were displayed at several Motoramas held around the country from 1949 to 1961. The Motoramas, which also displayed GM's "dream cars," were particularly popular in 1956 when 2.3 million people attended shows in five cities.

There was a tremendous growth in popularity of the OHV V-8 in the 1950's, led by the 265 cu. in. V-8 that Chevrolet introduced in its 1955 models. Though Cadillac and Oldsmobile had developed powerful OHV V-8s in 1949 the Chevrolet engine was a model of simplicity and efficiency, and was easily produced in large quantities. Extensive development work led to a V-8 that was 35 lbs. lighter and more powerful than the "stovebolt six." Available initially in 165 and 182 hp versions the engines powered Chevrolets to victory in several NASCAR events. The same engine also made the Corvette a successful competitor in road racing. The Chevrolet V-8 and the Pontiac V-8, introduced in 1957, made performance affordable, and like all of GM's V-8s, would inspire generations of powerful and reliable engines used in cars of all divisions through the 1960's and 1970's.

The 1951 Buick LeSabre (left top) and the 1951 XP-300 (below) had styling and engineering advances years ahead of their time. Harley Earl at the wheel of the LeSabre (left bottom). The 1956 GM Aerotrain (above) combined high speed with low operating costs.

Two of the most surprising participants in the 1950 LeMans 24 hour road race were a pair of Series 61 Cadillacs entered by American sportsman Briggs Cunningham. One, with a streamlined racing body, was nicknamed "Le Monstre" by the French and placed eleventh overall despite the loss of all gears except top. The other car was virtually stock (right); its potent OHV V-8, first introduced in 1949, allowed it to maintain an average speed of 81.33 mph for a tenth-place finish. For Oldsmobile 1950 was a year of performance as well. The twin innovations of 1949—Futuramic styling and the 303 cu. in. Rocket V-8—were carried over into 1950. Contributing to a division production record of 396,757 units was the attractive Holiday Deluxe hardtop (left); over 11,000 were built for the year. In 1950 Chevrolet's 4 door Bel Air Fastback (below) helped the division build more than two million units in a single year, shattering industry records. In the same year Chevrolet became the first U.S. automaker to offer an automatic transmission in the low-priced field.

The star of Cadillac's 1953 lineup was the limited edition Eldorado (left). Only 532 were built; all featured wraparound windshields, Cadillac's first, sloping belt line and special interiors in elegant leathers. The Eldorado continued in this form through 1955, whereupon it became an upper Cadillac series, still limited, for 1956 in both convertible and hardtop forms. It would gradually lead to the Eldorado Brougham of 1957–1960 and the front-wheel-drive Eldorados of the 1960's.

Buick celebrated its 50th anniversary in 1953 with its first production V-8 engine, the unique Skylark convertible (above) and its seven-millionth car, built in June of this year. Like the Eldorado the Skylark was a limited edition. It was inspired by the experimental Le Sabre, and with its top up, it was only 5 ft. high. Standard equipment on the Skylark included power windows, power brakes, power seats and a power aerial for the foot-controlled Selectronic radio. The owner's name was engraved on a gold-colored emblem plate on the hub of the steering wheel.

The year 1951 was the last for Chevrolet's fastbacks, and the second year for the stylish hardtops. The Bel Air Deluxe Coupe (below), like all other 1952 Chevrolets, was powered by the famous OHV six. A total of 74,634 models were sold this year.

With the XP-300 showcar as instigator and the production Skylark as a bellwether, all 1954 Buicks were crisp, clear and striking. The 1954 Super Convertible (right) helped bring Buick to third place in the industry with a calendar year production of 531,463 units. Cadillac's 1954 Coupe de Ville (near left) had impressive performance from its 230 hp V-8 with dual exhaust. The 1954 Pontiac Star Chief Custom Catalina (far left) was a refinement of the 1953 Chieftain. A total of 109 new features were included in the 1954 models, more than any other Pontiac since 1926.

CORVETTE

Designed in 1952 and displayed at GM's Motoramas the following year, the 1953 Chevrolet Corvette (left bottom) was destined to become America's premier sports car. Though not slated as a production car at its birth, the Corvette was so well received by the public that it was put into production in 1953. It was the first of three "dream" cars to reach production, along with the Chevrolet Nomad and Cadillac Eldorado Brougham.

With its trim lines, folding top and side curtains, the Corvette had the features of a true sports car. Its 235.5 cu. in., OHV, "Blue Flame" six featured aluminum pistons, 8.0:1 compression ratio and an output of 150 hp. Underneath its fiberglass body—the first use of the material in a production car—the Corvette rode on a modified X-frame chassis with a live axle suspended on elliptic springs. Its front suspension's parallel wishbone layout was derived from Chevrolet's full-size cars.

While the initial run of 319 Corvettes (all in Polo White) were virtually hand-assembled in Chevrolet's Flint, Michigan plant, Corvette production was soon transferred to a plant in St. Louis.

At its announcement the Corvette included a Powerglide automatic transmission, windshield washers, whitewall tires, a clock and a cigarette lighter. A novel innovation for the day was a red warning light that came on when the parking brake was applied.

With the imminent addition of a manual transmission and a V-8 engine, Corvette's 30 year tenure as America's only production sports car would be assured.

The year 1955 was a banner one for GM; U.S. production for the year topped an amazing 3.98 million units and helped GM increase its market share to over 50%. Chevrolet was clearly the leader of this sales boom; its 1955 models occupied nearly a quarter of the market by themselves. The 1955 Bel Air convertible (below) gave a youthful look to the line and was selected to pace that year's Indianapolis 500. A Bel Air 2 door hardtop (right bottom) came off the line as GM's fifty-millionth car. The Bel Air Nomad station wagon (left) featured unique curved rear windows. The division's newly developed 265 cu. in. V-8 proved especially popular with buyers and sired a series of light-weight and efficient V-8s that would power generations of Chevrolets to come.

Pontiac's Star Chief Custom Safari station wagon (right top) was a sister to Chevrolet's Nomad. The most exciting and luxurious wagon ever produced by the division, it helped boost Pontiac's production to a new high of over 580,000 cars.

Greyhound's 220 hp production Scenicruiser of 1954 (near left top) marked one of the great steps in the coach's evolution. It provided almost insurpassable luxurious comfort for 43 passengers riding high above car height and glareless, all-around visibility. Newly developed tension rubber shackles and tandem rear axles minimized road shock.

The 1960 GMC DLR 8000 light-weight semi-trailer (far left top) was built on a new high-tensile, steel-welded frame with air suspension and independent front wheels. It was GMC's entry into the light-weight custom-made cab which culminated with the Astro 95 in the 1970's.

The star of GM's 1955 Motorama was GMC's "L'Universelle" panel truck (left bottom), with driver's compartment forward of the front axle and a front-wheel-drive design, greatly lowering the load floor. (Right top) 1955 Pontiac Catalina, incorporating many of Pontiac's new styling features of the year: the wraparound windshield, cowl ventilation, Hydra-matic drive, 12 volt electrical system, Strato-Streak V-8, which was offered in 173 and 180 hp as well as a 200 hp power pack. Ninety percent of the 554,090 Pontiacs sold had the new Dual Range Hydra-matics.

The 1955 Chevrolet also offered a new V-8 and quickly earned the right to its slogan "the hot one." Virtually overnight this model changed Chevrolet's image, quickly capturing the youth market with its flashy performance and zestful styling. The new Chevrolet V-8 had a performance level and margin of surprising potential that attracted NASCAR efforts. The rakish styling showed the way to the light, pillarless hardtop with its graceful flowing line, teasingly hinting speed, and aligned itself further with the Italian eggcrate racing grille. All divisions introduced in 1956 a pillarless hardtop, inspired by the 1953 Cadillac showcar "Orleans." (Right bottom) 1956 4 door Chevrolet hardtop sedan.

CHEVROLET

In 1957 Chevrolet produced some cars that were destined to become milestones. It would be the last—and possibly the best—year for the new youthful look that was initiated in 1955. Fuel injection became available on the newly enlarged 283 cu. in. V-8; the top injected engine was capable of 283 hp from 283 cu. in., the first American engine to achieve "the engineer's dream."

The 1957 Chevrolet Bel Air Nomad (right bottom) remained the division's most expensive car. Just over 6000 were built. The 1957 Cameo Carrier (left) was another attractive offer from Chevrolet. A year earlier it had become America's first smooth-sided pickup. It was also the first pickup truck of its type to cater to both commercial and personal applications, with a large bed, V-8 power, comfortable interior and stylish trim. By the late 1950's the entire U.S. truck industry had followed Chevrolet's lead by introducing smooth-sided pickups. By 1956 the Chevrolet Corvette (right top) was coming into its own as the American sports car. The 185 hp, 265 cu. in. V-8 introduced in 1955 was upgraded to 210 hp. A 225 hp powerplant was optional. A three-speed manual transmission became standard equipment; Powerglide was optional. Also new for 1956 were roll-up windows and optional fiberglass hardtop and power-operated soft top. As it would for years to come the Corvette remained a limited edition model; only 3467 models were built during 1956.

Intended as both a rolling test bed and a serious competition car, the 1957 Corvette SS (far right top) was conceived by Chevrolet engineer Zora Arkus-Duntov. It featured a tubular frame, magnesium body, de Dion rear axle. A special option for 1957 production Corvettes, RPO 684, transformed the car into a serious racing machine. In 1957 a Corvette took the SCCA Class B Production Championship, beginning an eight-year span during which that category was dominated by Corvettes.

Pontiac's 1957 Bonneville Convertible (left) was available with a new fuel-injected 347 cu. in., 315 hp V-8. Fuel injection was exclusive to the Bonneville and only a few were so equipped. All Pontiacs for 1957 used the 347 cu. in. engine; levels of output ranged from a low compression 227 hp version to a NASCAR Tri-Power 347 that produced 317 hp.

The most luxurious American car for 1957 was the Cadillac Eldorado Brougham (above). Debuting at the 1957 Los Angeles International Auto Show the Eldorado Brougham, like the Chevrolet Corvette, was a "dream car come true." Only 400 1957 models and 304 1958 models were built, but all offered such unique features as a brushed stainless-steel roof, constant level air suspension system and quadruple headlights, with one pair used for city driving and both pairs for country driving. Oldsmobile celebrated its 60th anniversary in 1957 with its first station wagon since 1950. One version, the Super 88 wagon (right), featured hardtop styling similar to that on GM's new pillarless sedans. Power was supplied by the famous Rocket V-8 engine. All 1957 station wagons carried the familiar Fiesta nameplate.

For today's collectors the 1957 Chevrolet Bel Air convertible (near left) is a prized possession. Its clean lines were made a little crisper for the year, giving the car a longer look.

As on the Corvette fuel injection was available, though few "fuelies" were built. The most powerful carbureted V-8 for the year was the 270 hp version with a pair of four-barrel carburetors.

Equally attractive was the 1957 Bel Air Sport Coupe (below). In base form it was moderately priced and over 160,000 were built.

GMC's 1957 Palomino pickup (far left) was a one-off prototype, but its styling themes were used in production versions from both Chevrolet and GMC.

Cadillac pioneered the use of "tail fins" in 1948; a decade later they had reached their stylistic and practical limits. The fins on the 1959 Cadillac Eldorado Seville (right) made it one of the most controversial Cadillacs ever built; it was also one of the lowest in height.

Chevrolet introduced a new full-size line for 1958: the Impala. The top of the line was the Impala Sport Coupe (below). Standard on all 1958 Chevrolet models were full-coiled suspension and a "Safety Girder" frame.

Pontiac's 1959 models, with their new split grilles, aimed for a youthful image. Americans responded quickly to the new look by buying over 83,000 cars between September 1, 1957 and January 1, 1958.

Pontiac's 1959 Bonneville Vista hardtop sedan (left) featured the GM "blade" airfoil roof design that overhung the 180° panoramic rear window. The 1959 cars incorporated 47 engineering developments, including improved brakes and the soon-to-be-famous Wide-Track suspension that added 5 in. to the front and the rear tracks.

137

The year 1959 saw the end of the radical styling competition that had taken over the industry in the late 1950's. Chevrolet's Bel Air 2 door sedan (left) rode on a 119 in. wheelbase, making it the longest car in the low-priced field. It was also 3 in. wider than its 1958 predecessor and offered five more inches of interior width as a result of thinner doors.

Engines available for 1959 included a 235 cu. in. six, and 283 and 348 cu. in. V-8s. A fuel-injected version of the 283 was capable of 315 hp. A new model for 1959 was the El Camino, which combined elements of passenger car and pickup truck. The Impala line, a subset of the Bel Air line in 1958, became its own series in 1959. Over 70,000 Impalas contributed to Chevrolet's production of 1.48 million 1959 cars. All Chevrolets for the year rode on a new X-frame chassis; the design afforded both strength and rigidity and allowed the body to be lower than ever before.

The first public glimpse of the redesigned 1963 Corvette came not at an auto show but at a racetrack. Starting in 1958 GM stylist Bill Mitchell began crafting a body for a leftover Corvette SS frame and entered the car, known as the "Sting Ray," in competition. Debuting at the President's Cup race at Maryland's Marlboro Raceway in April 1959 the Sting Ray (above) was the center of attention and placed fourth in the race. At the end of its first season the car was completely overhauled, with a refurbished body and improved brakes. After several successful track appearances in 1960 the Sting Ray was rebuilt once again and put on the auto show circuit beginning with Chicago's McCormick Place in February 1961. The stunning new Corvette Sting Ray that debuted in the fall of the following year would share many of the same design themes as the original 1959 Sting Ray racer.

139

GM'S MOTORAMAS, SHOWCARS, AND EXPERIMENTALS

GM had constantly been at work on technical and styling innovations, some of which would eventually work their way into production cars. But much of what went on in the Styling Section was understandably confidential. In the late 1940's, however, it was decided that the scope of the work underway there was such that it deserved to be shown to the public. In addition the displays would allow GM to gauge public interest in new ideas.

GM's first exhibition entitled "Transportation Unlimited," opened at New York's Waldorf Astoria Hotel in January 1949. Attendance there and at a subsequent show in Boston topped half a million people. The New York show the following year drew over 300,000. After a two-year hiatus, the exhibition returned in 1953 as the General Motors' Motorama, and toured in Miami, Los Angeles, San Francisco, Dallas and Kansas City in addition to New York. Attendance for that year swelled to a million and a half.

GM's Motoramas proved popular with the public for several reasons. In addition to dozens of experimental and production cars showcased in elaborate displays, the Motoramas featured orchestras and troupes of dancers who would perform at half-hour intervals. As a result the Motoramas required extensive preparation. Over 100 trucks were used to transport the cars and displays around the country, and the complexity of the shows demanded that each truck had to arrive at a precise time and in a specific order.

GM's Motoramas ran until 1961, and though there was not always a show every year, attendance for all shows from 1949 to 1961 was over ten million. The Motoramas were ultimately discontinued, a result of their increasingly high costs and declining popularity—a factor effected by television. Another reason for ending the Motoramas was that they provided the competition with a glimpse into GM's future and the public was polled not only by GM market researchers but by other manufacturers as well.

The 1954 Oldsmobile Experimental F-88 (far left top) was a 2 seater sports model, incorporating a panoramic windshield, then a recent innovation. Jet airfoil wheel discs were used to cool the brakes, and performance was monitored by aircraft style instrumentation. Powering the F-88 was a 250 hp, 325 cu. in. V-8 with Hydra-matic transmission.

The Oldsmobile Starfire (far left bottom) debuted at the 1953 GM Motorama. The 2 seater roadster also featured a LeSabre-style panoramic windshield that would become a production feature on all 1954 and 1955 GM cars.

The 1954 Buick Wildcat II (left center top) constructed of fiberglass, was just under 4 ft. high. The hood mascot, naturally, was a "wild cat." The car's standard 322 cu. in. Buick V-8 engine utilized four carburetors to provide 220 hp. Dual spotlights were mounted on the doors.

The Wildcat theme evolved into the Wildcat III in 1955 (near left top), an open 4 seater. Styling was closely related to 1955 production Buicks, but the engine was a special "four carb" version that was capable of 280 hp.

The 1954 Oldsmobile Cutlass (left center) was the ultimate in hardtops in its day. It featured a radio-telephone between the seats and a unique "venetian blind" treatment for the rear windows that would later become popular on several fastback designs.

Cadillac's LaSalle II (near left center), displayed at GM's 1955 Motorama, comprised many technical innovations. Its V-6 engine was fuel-injected and produced 150 hp. The car's aluminum wheels had brake drums cast integrally and were designed to be self-cooling. Exhaust pipes were routed through the lower body sills and exited just ahead of the rear body sills.

As a result of the tremendous interest in the Corvette GM Styling produced a host of derivatives, among them the 1954 Nomad station wagon (near left bottom). Following the Corvette's lead the Nomad went into production, with slight changes, as the 1955 Chevrolet Bel Air Nomad. The showcar was powered by a 6 cyl. engine with automatic transmission, but the production Nomad was available with Chevrolet's potent 265 cu. in. OHV V-8.

141

GM's 1956 Motorama featured some of the
most alluring dream cars ever built. For that
year shows appeared in New York, Miami,
Los Angeles, San Francisco and Boston.
Total attendance at all the 1956 Motoramas
was over 2.3 million.

Pontiac's 1956 Club de Mer (near right top)
was designed for open air motoring. Just over
3 ft. high and 15 ft. long the Club de Mer was
powered by a 300 hp Strato-Streak V-8. It
also featured a rear-mounted gearbox and a de
Dion rear axle. Headlights were hidden within
rotating housings.

The 1956 Buick Centurion (center top) was
another popular attraction of this year's
Motorama. An aerodynamically designed 4
seater the Centurion used a rear-mounted TV
camera in place of a rearview mirror. Seats
were designed with several passenger conve-
nience features including front seats that
automatically slid backward when the doors
were opened, and also moved forward to
allow easier entry and exit for rear seat
passengers. A further innovation was a can-
tilever-suspended steering wheel inspired by
aircraft designs. The steering column was
located on the centerline of the car, giving the
driver more leg room.

Oldsmobile's 1956 Golden Rocket (near
right bottom) debuted alongside the Club de
Mer at the Motorama. Like the Centurion it
featured a special seating system. As the door
was opened the roof panel was raised while
the seat was elevated and rotated toward the
passenger or driver. Two buttons located on
the steering wheel, which incorporated a
speedometer, allowed it to tilt downward,
providing the driver with greater access. The
Golden Rocket utilized a 275 hp "Rocket" V-8.

The turbine-powered Firebird II (far right)
was presented at the 1956 Miami Motorama.
The Cadillac El Camino (center) first displayed in 1954, was a companion to the
convertible La Espada. Unique from a material standpoint was the El Camino's fiberglass
body and brushed stainless-steel top. The
curved glass used in the aircraft-type bubble
canopy conformed to the roof contours, enhanced the crisp, clean lines of the car. Power
came from a 1954 Cadillac OHV V-8.

GM's trio of experimental Firebirds (left) tested the practicality of gas turbine engines for passenger car use as well as acting as testbeds for a host of new concepts in transportation. The first Firebird, the 1954 XP-21 (far left), was America's first gas turbine automobile and used a GM-built 370 hp engine. The 1956 Firebird II (left center), a 4 seater, used a 200 hp unit. It featured a titanium outer skin, the first use of the material in an automobile body, and a self-leveling hydro-pneumatic suspension system. The 1959 Firebird III (near left and below) was even more advanced and included features that eventually went into production cars, such as cruise control, constant temperature air conditioning system, and a special anti-skid braking system. Inspired by the svelte jet fighters of the late 1950's Cadillac's 1959 Cyclone (right) had a retractable plastic canopy, coated from within with vaporized silver, that lifted automatically when a door was opened. The doors themselves did not swing out, but rather slid alongside the body when opened. Radar sensors placed in the nosecones at the tip of each fender warned of approaching objects and a two-way intercom allowed passengers to speak with outsiders without opening the canopy. The Cyclone was displayed at the 1959 Motorama.

CHAPTER SEVEN

MARKETING OF PERFORMANCE

1960-1969

The 1960's were years of refinement and growth, and the tremendous changes that were to take place would manifest themselves early in the decade. In the two model years that followed 1960 the exuberance that characterized the late 1950's was transformed into a feeling of sensible functionalism.

The first example of this coming trend was the compact Chevrolet Corvair. New interest in compact cars was catered to again in 1961, when GM's A-body cars debuted: Buick's Skylark, Oldsmobile's F-85 and Pontiac's Tempest. Though these cars shared several internal components, each had unique external identification and a unique powerplant. The Chevrolet Chevelle, which also shared the A-body chassis, was introduced in 1964.

Buick's 1963 Riviera was a trendsetter in styling as well as concept. Its continental lines, combined with advanced engine and suspension research, created GM's first personalized touring car of the 1960's. The concept of a personal luxury car would soon spread to other divisions, creating the Pontiac Grand Prix, and the front-wheel-drive Cadillac Eldorado and Oldsmobile Toronado. The Riviera was a styling inspiration, and would be emulated throughout the auto industry in the 1960's.

The Chevrolet Corvette, America's only production sports car for the decade, continued to grow in popularity through the 1960's. Model year production grew from 12,508 in 1960 to 27,540 in 1969. The Corvette was completely restyled in 1963 and 1969 with both coupe and convertible versions available.

Appealing to a broader market were the Chevrolet Camaro and Pontiac Firebird. Both were destined to satisfy the growing interest in moderately priced personal "sporty" cars. Both were available in coupe or convertible form, and could be equipped with 6 or 8 cyl. engines.

Technical developments were frequent in the decade,

particularly engine research. The OHV V-8s, pioneered by Cadillac in 1949 and available in all divisions in 1957, provided a firm base for further engine development. In 1962 Buick developed a 215 cu. in., aluminum block V-8 for its new Special; the first GM all-aluminum V-8. It weighed substantially less than iron block 4 cyl. engines, yet produced 140 hp. Oldsmobile added a turbocharger and fuel injection to the engine, installed it in its new F-85 in 1962 and called the car the Jetfire. Chevrolet enlarged the original 265 cu. in. V-8 once more in 1963 to create the famous 327, an engine that would be as well-known for its durability as its potency. Enlarged to 350 cu. in. in 1969 it powers the 1983 Impala, Caprice and Corvette.

New 6 cyl. engines were developed as well. Buick introduced a compact 225 cu. in. V-6 in 1964. Pontiac introduced an OHC six in 1966. In "sprint" form it produced 207 hp from 230 cu. in.

On the upper end of the performance spectrum was the musclecar, exemplified by the Pontiac GTO. By mating a Pontiac 389 cu. in. V-8 with a light-weight Tempest Le Mans body, Pontiac created a fast automobile with good road manners and a moderate price. Over 32,000 were sold in 1964, its first year. The concept was soon adopted by other divisions, creating the Chevelle SS 396, Oldsmobile 4-4-2 and the Buick Gran Sport.

With more distinct product lines in each division than ever before, each catering to a specific segment of the market, GM reached record levels in production and sales. GM's seventy-five-millionth car was produced in March 1962; the year also saw the number of shareholders in the corporation climb to over 1,000,000. The GM Futurama at the New York World's Fair welcomed over 29 million visitors in 1963 and 1964. In April 1967 GM built its one-hundred-millionth car, capping a successful decade.

1960 Buick LeSabre convertible.

By 1960 the famous Cadillac tailfin had begun to recede, allowing for smoother more fluid lines. The 1960 Cadillac line offered 13 models in three standard and one custom series. The 1960 Eldorado (near left top) was available in 15 standard and 5 special colors.

Oldsmobile's most popular line for 1960 was the Dynamic 88 series (near left bottom). The distinctive Dynamic 88 Holiday Sport Sedan made it the second most popular 88 model for the year with a production run of 43,761 cars. All 88s were powered by a 240 hp Rocket V-8.

Buick for 1960 boasted a series of technical developments. Separate heater controls for front and rear seats were available, the "Mirromagic" instrument panel allowed the driver to adjust the instrument dials and the Twilight Sentinel automatically turned the headlights on at dusk.

The Buick Invicta Estate Wagon (far left bottom) was new to the line for 1960. Power came from a 401 cu. in., 255 hp V-8. Buick, Oldsmobile and Pontiac collaborated in the development of a new "A-body" compact, each with its own unique powertrain and divisional identification. Buick cars were the Special and Skylark (far left top). The engine of the Buicks, an all-aluminum, 215 cu. in. V-8, was in part the result of research done on the all-aluminum engines used in the experimental Buick LeSabre and XP-300. It was one of the first production aluminum block V-8s in the country. The Special used a 155 hp version, while the Skylark featured a tweaked 185 hp version. A new optional automatic transmission was developed for the engine. Called the Dual Path Turbine Drive it was a combination of the Buick torque converter and planetary gearing, resulting in a transmission better in performance and economy than any earlier design.

Slightly downsized for 1961 the Pontiac full-size line, highlighted by the beautiful Bonneville convertible (right), proved popular. Pontiac V-8s were standard in all full-size cars, and ranged from a 389 cu. in. economy engine to a limited production 373 hp Super Duty 421 cu. in. engine. Unique options for 1961 were eight-lug aluminum hubs with integral drums. Pontiacs proved highly successful at stock car races around the country with 21 wins in 52 NASCAR events.

The 1962 Holden EJ model (far left top), completely restyled and extensively tested at the new GMH Lang Lang Proving Grounds, was powered by a 75 bhp, 138 cu. in. six, and a 3 speed manual transmission with Synchro-Mesh on second and third. Optional was the 3 speed Hydra-matic transmission. The EJ model celebrated Holden's millionth car and introduced Australia's first luxury car, the 4 door Premier.

Standard on all models were seat belts, a fully padded instrument panel and Duo-Servo hydraulic brakes. Both the transmission and steering box were lubricated for life. The windshield was curved, and the front sloping pillars improved visibility adding to the overall straight-through look. During the first year 154,811 EJs were built. In 1963 the "six" output was increased and a choice of three engines offering 95, 149 and 179 bhp were available.

(Near left top) Vauxhall's VAL bus, an unconventional but successful approach using a Twin-steer, 3 axle configuration with 16 in. wheels, attracted many builders. Illustrated is a Plaxton-bodied VAL.

(Left bottom) 1961 Bedford TK truck. In the 1960's TK models established Bedford among the leading truck builders. The TK engine, instead of being placed alongside the driver inside the cab, was placed in its own compartment underneath the driver. Advantages of this placement included an increase in space and comfort, and a reduction in noise. Other features of the TK Series were 16 in. wheels, available right up to the 5 tonners, which gave an entry step height as low as 19 in.

Vauxhall's new Victors of 1961 (right top), with 4 cyl., 1508 cc engines, ushered in the first VX 4/90 variant—a twin carburetor version with 44% more power. This extra performance 4 cyl. model gave effortless 90+ mph performance with the introduction of a 97.4 cu. in. engine developing 85.5 bhp at 5200 rpm. Bedford has traditionally gained a reputation in the four-wheel-drive field, supplying the armed forces of many countries with sturdy vehicles. (Right bottom) Bedford TJ Model of 1961.

On October 2, 1959 Chevrolet introduced the Corvair. A pioneer in technology the Corvair boasted such innovations as a rear-mounted, 140 cu. in., 6 cyl., air-cooled engine, producing 90 hp, and the first 4 wheel independent suspension in any GM automobile. The location of the engine made for greater traction and nearly equalized braking power front and rear. The engine and transaxle were combined in a light-weight unit which permitted a virtually unobstructed floor front and rear.

The Corvair was nine years in development and marked Chevrolet's entry into a distinctively new car class. It gained rapid public acceptance The 1961 Lakewood Station Wagon (right bottom) offered 58 cu. ft. of storage space behind the front seat and 10 cu. ft. under the hood—more cargo space than other compact wagons and even more than some larger cars.

In 1962 Chevrolet expanded on its two legendary engines, which were first introduced in 1955. The first, a small block V-8 displacing 327 cu. in., was available in 250 and 300 hp versions. Lighter than the same year's 235.5 cu. in. six, it would remain in the Chevrolet line until 1968. The second engine, a 409 cu. in. V-8, was installed in 1962 Bel Airs (left) and Impalas, leading the way to the first real "musclecars." The 409, which was available with as much as 409 hp, powered Chevrolet to several victories in stock car and drag racing.

Pontiac's full-size line for 1962 included dozens of new features for the year, including improved intake manifolds, redesigned carburetors and a modified front suspension layout that permitted a tighter turning radius and a new "Cushion Flex" ride. The 1962 Catalina 2 door hardtop (right top) could be ordered with a "Super Duty" 421 cu. in. engine with dual four-barrel carburetors that produced 405 hp.

The Corvair Monza series of showcars are among the most exalted prototypes ever produced by GM's Styling Section. The Corvair Monza GT, which debuted at the 1962 New York Auto Show (above and below), was derived from the successful production Corvair Monza. The Monza GT featured a mid-mounted, air-cooled, 6 cyl. powerplant that was placed ahead of the rear axle. Its suspension was carried on tubular steel extensions and was fully independent. The fiber- and plexiglass cockpit cover was designed to combine windshield, doors and roof into one unit and swung forward, allowing for easier entry and exit. While the seats were fixed, pedals were adjustable. Ventilation was through fresh air ducts at the base of the windshield. The Venetian blind louvers at the rear window controlled rearward vision and airflow. Air was inducted into the engine through openings in front of the rear wheels. Wheelbase was 92 in., track was 53 in. and height was 42 in.

The Corvair Monza SS (right) was a topless version of the GT, with a low-cut windscreen that encircled the driver. Unlike the GT the Corvair SS had its engine placed behind the rear axle in typical Corvair fashion. Its wheelbase, at 88 in., was 4 in. shorter than the GT's.

The 1963 Buick Riviera (near left) was designed with a continental elegance never before seen on an American car. It inspired the 1963 Silver Arrow (far left), a showcar that lost none of the Riviera's beauty. The Silver Arrow was said to have combined elements of the Rolls-Royce and Ferrari. Indeed the Silver Arrow has a taut, lean look, with a sharply sculptured roofline, sheer side panels, a low silhouette and unique frameless side windows. Few changes were made to the Riviera for 1964 (below); the 425 cu. in., 340 hp engine that was optional in 1963 was made standard equipment in 1964—a second four-barrel carburetor, which boosted output even further, was optional.

The 1963 Corvette Sting Ray (right) was the development of a body design first seen on the 1959 Sting Ray racer. The new car sported an entirely redesigned body, along with a fully independent suspension system. Both convertible and coupe versions were available; the split rear window treatment was done only in 1963 making it one of the most desirable Corvettes for collectors.

The Chevrolet Chevelle, introduced in 1964, was the division's third new line in four years, giving it a total of five lines, each catering to a different segment of the market. The Chevelle's sporty lines and moderate price made it immediately appealing to young Americans. The 1964 Chevelle SS (left) was the top Chevelle for the year. The SS equipment package included individual front bucket seats, engine gauges and special SS insignia.

Chevrolet broke daily, weekly, monthly and model year production records in 1963. It also built its fifty-millionth car, which New York Governor Nelson Rockefeller drove off the line at Chevrolet's Tarrytown assembly plant on June 10, 1963. Returning for its second year in 1963 was the compact Chevy II (right). The car's unitized body was like nothing else ever produced by Chevrolet. Two new engines were available for the Chevy II, a 153 cu. in. four, producing 90 hp, and a 194 cu. in. six with 120 hp. The 1963 Pontiac Grand Prix (below) prefaced a generation of "personalized" cars soon to come. The Grand Prix was introduced in 1962, but was totally restyled for 1963 with crisper lines and a minimum of side trim. A 389 cu. in. V-8 was standard, but buyers could opt for a Tri-Power 412 cu. in. "High Output" V-8 with three two-barrel carburetors.

The coupling of Pontiac's big-block V-8 and the mid-size Tempest Le Mans in 1964 created the legendary Pontiac GTO (below). The GTO package included such extras as heavy-duty suspension, quick ratio power steering, dual exhausts and red-stripe tires. Consumer reaction to the first GTO was so strong that an initial limit of 5000 cars was lifted and 32,450 were eventually produced, making the GTO the best-selling first-year car ever produced by the division.

Chevrolet's 1964 Impala SS 409 (right), with either 400 or 425 hp on tap, was the division's top performer for that year. The 409 took Chevrolet to a Class I victory in the Pure Oil Performance Trials in 1964; Chevrolet models took first place in four other categories as well.

The millionth Corvair, a Monza Spyder Convertible, was produced in 1964. The Monza lineup, which also included 4 door sedan and Club Coupe (left) models, continued to be the most popular Corvair series, with a 1964 model year production of 141,400.

In the 1960's GM produced several advanced design turbine-powered trucks. The aerodynamically designed gas turbine Bison (left), an experimental freight hauler conceived by GM's Styling Section, was first shown at the 1964 New York World's Fair. The integrated, rigid, interlocking, weatherproof containers, easily detachable for transfer, could also form a separate cargo trailer with its own rear wheels and dolly when coupled together in sets. The Bison's twin 1000 hp turbine powerplant was mounted in a pod behind the cab to form a closed aerodynamic link between the tractor and trailer roof. One turbine of 300 hp provided propulsion for normal highway driving; the other, a 700 hp, was on call for accelerating and climbing grades under heavy load. The cab's design was functional as well as aesthetic. Its aerodynamic styling reduced cab noise, and its single panoramic wraparound windshield provided uninterrupted vision to the operator. (Right) 1965 Chevrolet Turbo Titan III. The "Truck of Tomorrow" embodied fiberglass and steel space-age design and was powered by a GT-309 gas turbine of 280 hp, an engine that had evolved from over 15 years of research and development. Three years prior to the Titan an identical engine had been tested in a conventional Chevy truck. The GT-309 was smaller and about one-third as heavy as a comparably powered Diesel engine. The Titan's cab was fitted with astronaut seats and was the first to offer in any truck a four-speaker FM stereo radio and two-way radio telephone. Other innovations included power swing-up windows controlled by the door key, a pedestal-mounted steering console with horizontal twin-dial steering, retractable turn signals and square-lens triple headlamps mounted vertically with a special turnpike beam at the bottom. Air was drawn through this area for the turbine. The Titan III marked the first time Chevrolet had built a special vehicle to test the gas turbine.

The sleek, compact sports coupe that appeared on the Opel stand at the 1965 Frankfurt Auto Show turned many heads. The GT, itself a dream car derivative, was the first modern "sports" car from Opel, as well as the first European example of the popular American dream car concept. With the production of the new Kadett in late 1967 the Opel GT (above) became a production reality, riding on the Kadett chassis with either a 1.1 or 1.9 liter 4 cyl. engine. From 1968 to 1973 over 100,000 of the rakish coupes were built, with 60% of production destined for America, where they were sold through Buick dealers.

First available on the 1961 Chevrolet Impalas, Chevrolet's "SS" option package soon became popular on Novas and Chevelles as well. The new look of the 1965 Chevrolets made them among the division's most attractive cars in the decade. The SS package on the 1965 Impala (right) included front bucket seats divided by a console that housed a rally-style clock. Though the base engine was a 230 cu. in. six, two new 396 cu. in. V-8's became available mid-year—one was rated at 325 hp, the other at 425.

The Buick Riviera (below) was further refined for 1965; the headlights had retractable covers, like the Silver Arrow, and the taillights were integrated into the rear bumper. It was only natural that elements of the clean Riviera design would find their way into the rest of the Buick line; in 1965 roof lines were more sloping, hoods were lower and rear decks were shorter. A new Gran Sport version of the Riviera was offered for the year. Heading the list of Gran Sport features were a 360 hp version of the 425 cu. in. V-8, a specially calibrated transmission and a positive traction rear axle. A ride and handling option included a faster steering ratio and heavy-duty suspension and rear track bar bushings.

Pontiac's widely admired GTO entered its third year in 1967, and sales of "The Tiger" topped 96,000 units. A pair of new engine options were available that year. Performance-minded buyers could opt for a 360 hp, 400 cu. in. V-8. On the other end of the scale was an economy version of the engine with a two-barrel carburetor and an output of 255 hp. A 1966 convertible is pictured at left.

New for 1966 from Vauxhall was a luxury version of the Vauxhall PC (right). Called the Viscount it featured power steering, electric windows and automatic transmission.

Buick's 1966 Sportwagon (below), originally introduced in 1964, featured a Skyroof, which was shared by Oldsmobile and was unique to the automotive world—no other cars had this raised roof.

167

After an extensive testing program that had begun in 1959 Oldsmobile introduced the front-wheel-drive Toronado (left bottom) in 1966. It was a handsome car from any angle, with an individual look that emphasized its sporty, personal car character. Power was derived from a 425 cu. in. V-8 engine.

Chevrolet's successful "Super Sports" concept was applied to several of its cars throughout the 1960's and 1970's. In 1966 Impalas were available with SS equipment in both convertible and coupe versions (far left top). All Impalas were restyled for 1966. SS models included Strato-bucket front seats; engine options ranged from a 250 cu. in. six to a 425 hp Mark IV 427 V-8.

Both the 1961 Mako Shark and its 1965 successor, the Mako Shark II (near left top), were functioning testbeds for production Corvettes. The original Mako Shark, which was inspired by the experimental XP-720, was designed in 1961, and after considerable track and wind tunnel testing, was displayed at the 1962 New York Auto Show. The Mako Shark influenced the styling of the 1963 Corvette. Similarly the Mako Shark II anticipated the 1968 Corvette.

Cadillac's Eldorado saw its final year in rear-drive form in 1966 (right top). It was also the last Eldorado convertible version to be produced until 1971. During 1966 205,001 Cadillacs were produced.

GM's sportiest new automobile for 1967 was the Chevrolet Camaro. Proportioned in a long, low silhouette, the Camaro featured a long hood line and a relatively short rear deck. Computer technology was employed during the car's development, and extensive ride and handling developmental tests were performed on the new model. Underneath, its unit body construction and single leaf rear spring offered excellent ride and handling characteristics.

The SS 350 Camaro (right bottom) with available Rally Sport package was 1967's top-of-the-line Camaro. The SS option included such extras as stronger suspension components, D70 x 14 Wide Oval red-stripe tires on special 6 in. rims and chrome-plated engine trim. A total of 220,900 Camaros were produced in 1967.

The 1967 Buick fastback Riviera (left) featured an all-new 430 cu. in. engine shared with the division's Wildcat and Electra models. Rivieras used their own X-frame design with a strong central section and no outer rails.

Cadillac's front-wheel-drive luxury car, the Eldorado, was introduced in 1967. New for 1968 (below) was a 472 cu. in. V-8, then the largest displacement of any V-8 in the industry. The Eldorado's front-wheel-drive system had such superior traction that one test engineer was able to drive a prototype over ice at twice the speed possible with a conventional rear-wheel-drive car. Buick's 1968 Wildcat (right) was available with special side trim. Buick production at Flint set a record for 1968 of 350,826 cars.

The Chevrolet Corvette (left), America's "star-spangled sports car," had its body redesigned for 1968. In addition to its restyling the Corvette's most obvious new features were a pair of lift-off roof panels that gave the open-air effect of a convertible. A convertible and a removable hardtop version were also available.

Other new features on the 1968 Corvette included a fiber-optic light monitoring device with a console-mounted display showing the status of all exterior lamps. When not in use the Corvette's windshield wipers were safely hidden under a vacuum-operated panel at the base of the windshield. Engine availability went from a 300 hp 327 cu. in. V-8 to a 435 hp 427 cu. in. V-8.

The Pontiac GTO, America's first "musclecar," was entering its third year in 1968 (right bottom). New on the 1968 GTO was a special "Endura" front end, a one-piece flexible body cover nose cap that integrated the bumper with the body. The GTO's wheelbase was reduced by 3 in. to 112 in., and overall car length was decreased by 6 in. A new frame was added, and side guard door beams were installed to comply with recent government safety standards. The rear axle featured a new four-link suspension system that was designed to control axle hop under hard acceleration.

Chevrolet's Blazer (right top), introduced in 1969, helped create a new demand for four-wheel-drive vehicles. Use of multi-leaf, two-stage springs all around allowed for a comfortable ride with excellent ground clearance. Available power steering and brakes, a fiberglass hardtop as well as heavy-duty clutch and suspension packages made further on- and off-the-road usage possible.

Chevrolet's Impala series, first introduced in 1958, had become the division's most popular series a decade later. Over 770,000 1969 models (right top) were built.

The 1969 Opel Aero GT coupe (left), first shown at the Frankfurt Auto Show of the same year, was a proposed successor to the highly successful Opel GT. A removable "targa" panel covered the passenger compartment and the rear window could be lowered electrically.

Pontiac's sporty Grand Prix became more individual in 1969, sharing few body panels with the division's other cars. While a 400 cu. in., 370 hp V-8 was standard, the Grand Prix SJ (right bottom) included a 428 cu. in., 370 hp V-8, special gauges and an automatic leveling system.

It was the last year for the Chevrolet Corvair in 1969 (below). GM's first compact of the 1960's had a nine-year production of 1.7 million cars and over 79,000 trucks. The Corvair was a truly unique product.

175

CHAPTER EIGHT

THE YEARS OF TRANSITION

1970-1979

The 1970's began on a theme of performance and ended on one of fuel economy. By the mid 1970's drastic changes in automobile design were dictated not only by increasing federal involvement in the auto industry but also by the 1974 energy crisis and the growing number of imported automobiles. GM quickly adapted to these new challenges, beginning with the subcompact Chevrolet Vega in 1971, and near the end of the decade, with a lineup of automobiles symbolized by the X-cars, a new line of front-wheel-drive vehicles that provided increased fuel efficiency but little sacrifice in comfort or performance.

The "musclecar" reached the pinnacle of its development in 1970. With the exception of Cadillac each division offered big-block engines with ultra high performance in mid-size automobiles. By 1971, however, the government's growing concern over exhaust emissions and safety, along with the reluctance of the nation's insurance companies to offer policies for high performance cars, saw horsepower figures drop dramatically. Another factor reducing output was an across the board decision in 1971 that all GM engines operate on unleaded gasoline in preparation for the catalytic converters, an emission control device that would be standard on all GM cars in 1975. The use of the unleaded fuel led to a necessary reduction in compression ratios and thus horsepower.

The first GM car to be designed from the ground up with the 1970's in mind was the Chevrolet Vega. In many ways the Vega's design and construction prefaced that of cars to come. The Vega was the first American car to make extensive use of computerized robots to perform repetitive tasks such as spot welding. The Vega was also designed to be maintained by owners, with a detailed repair manual explaining most basic repairs.

The fuel crisis in 1974 demanded a new emphasis on fuel economy for GM. The first response was the 1976 Chevrolet Chevette, which became the most fuel efficient American-built car in the country. The pre-eminent importance of fuel efficiency spread to large cars as well. Cadillac introduced its first "small" car in 1975, the Seville. It was nearly 1000 lbs. lighter than the Coupe de Ville of the same year, yet maintained traditional Cadillac levels of comfort and performance. A year later GM's B- and C-car projects entered production, and like the Seville, the new GM models shed several hundred pounds, but sacrificed little interior space.

Closing out the decade was the X-car front-wheel-drive development program. The X-car was a new compact design, offering the traction and packaging advantages of front-wheel-drive in a car that had room for five adults and provided economy of over 20 mpg in city driving from a 2.5 liter, 4 cyl. engine. Introduced in early 1979 the X-car was offered by all GM divisions except Cadillac.

The 1970's would also have its share of milestones and anniversaries. Vauxhall would celebrate the construction of its one-millionth Viva model in 1971; in the same year Oldsmobile began manufacturing the sheet molding plastic compounds that would increasingly replace steel in several automotive components. Oldsmobile would also celebrate its 75th anniversary the following year.

GM of Canada produced its ten-millionth vehicle in 1975. The same year saw the production of the one-millionth Pontiac Grand Prix. Cadillac's 75th anniversary in 1977 coincided with a record fourth-quarter distribution of $928 million in shareholder dividends. Buick marked its 75th anniversary the following year.

By the end of the decade high fuel costs combining with increased foreign competition foreshadowed an entirely new automobile marketplace. Starting in 1979 GM would begin introducing a new generation of automobiles to meet the demands of the coming decade.

The Pontiac Trans Am (above) and the Chevrolet Camaro Z-28 (above top) had shapely new bodies for 1970. The Trans Am, with many performance features standard, used a 400 cu. in. Ram Air V-8 of 330 hp, while the Z-28 utilized a 360 hp, 350 cu. in. V-8.

Chevrolet's hot SS equipment package, available on the 1970 Camaro, Nova, Chevelle and new Monte Carlo, continued to be popular. The 1970 Nova SS 396 (below) was a rare version of the car. Most were equipped with 350 cu. in. V-8s producing 300 hp.

The 1970 Monte Carlo (right) was Chevrolet's answer to the personal luxury cars offered by other GM divisions. It had the longest hood of any Chevrolet ever built. Power came from a 455 cu. in. V-8. First-year production topped 130,000 units.

Starting in July 1969 GM-Holden's Research and Development and Advanced Styling Groups joined hands to design a limited production 2 seater sports car that could be manufactured on low-cost tooling. An all-fiberglass body, mounted on a full steel frame, was chosen. The use of fiberglass for the body permitted complete styling freedom. After numerous studies the GTR-X (far left top) emerged; a car of clean aerodynamic styling with a long, sleek hood and concealed headlights, low wedge-shape body and attractive rear end styling, enhanced by an elevated taillight assembly.

Mechanically the GTR-X used an independent front suspension with coil springs and upper and lower control arms; a live axle, with four links and coil springs, was used at the rear. Disc brakes were used on all four wheels. Powering the GTR-X was a 3 liter OHV six with triple carburetors. Power output was 190 hp at 5200 rpm. The transmission was a 4 speed manual version.

Also from GM-Holden's was the 1969 Hurricane (left bottom), a special research vehicle designed to test the viability of mid-engined, high-performance, sports/luxury cars. Power came from a GMH-designed, 253 cu. in. V-8. Suspension was fully independent front and rear, with trailing arms, lower lateral links and coil springs at the rear, and double "A" arms with coil springs at the front. Double U-joints were used on the driveshafts to the rear wheels. The canopy covering the Hurricane's cockpit was hinged on parallel links. For easier access to the 39 in. high car the seats rose up when the canopy was opened. Instrumentation was handled by cathode ray tube displays, while a rear-mounted television camera with a console-mounted monitor replaced the rear view mirror. The Hurricane debuted at the 1969 Melbourne Motor Show.

On the production front Vauxhall entered the 1970's with the successful Viva range (near left top). The standard engine was a 1.1 liter unit, with a 1.6 liter powerplant optional. The one-millionth Viva was built at the Luton, England plant on July 20, 1971. Dealer Team Vauxhall was also formed in 1971 to promote the use of Vauxhall cars in motorsport. The Viva remained in production from 1970 until mid 1979.

Vauxhall's experimental car (right) was the 1970 Special Research Vehicle (SRV). A 4 door, 4 seat prototype, the SRV was intended to act as a rolling test bed for research in the areas of suspension and engine design as well as aerodynamics. The SRV was fitted with a specially designed DOHC, 2 liter, 4 cyl. Vauxhall engine. The car's suspension was unique in design; a de Dion axle was used at the rear, while a beam axle riding on coil springs was employed at the front. Disc brakes were used on all four wheels.

GM produced over 4.8 million cars in the U.S. in 1971, close to the 1965 record of 4.9 million. Oldsmobile production totalled 775,191 units that year. The 1971 Olds Toronado (left) underwent its first major design change since 1966. It remained a front-wheel-drive car, but a new full frame featured four-link coil suspension at the rear, with shock absorbers mounted ahead of the axle. A 455 cu. in. V-8 was the only engine offered, with an output of 265 hp from larger valves, cold air induction and dual exhausts. Overall length was increased by 5.2 in. to 219.9 in., and the wheelbase was lengthened by 3 in.

The performance version of the Olds Cutlass for 1971 was the 4-4-2 (right center). Two 455 cu. in. V-8s were offered, a 340 hp version and a special W-30 350 hp package. Standard on the W-30 was a new double-disc clutch with a 4 speed manual transmission. A 3 speed automatic was also available. Zero to sixty mph for either version took just over 6 sec.

Cadillac's 1971 lineup was completely redesigned. Dropped was the Coupe de Ville convertible, replaced by a convertible version of the Eldorado. To comply with new federal safety standards all Cadillacs received stronger front ends with reinforced bumpers. The coming use of lead-free gasoline would lead to a reduction in the compression ratio of both the 472 cu. in. V-8 used in all Cadillacs except the Eldorado, and the Eldorado's 500 cu. in. V-8.

The 1972 Cadillac Fleetwood 60 Special Brougham (right top) had a redesigned front end with new lighting arrangements and a new grille.

Chevrolet took the number one sales slot in 1971 with 2.3 million cars sold. Leading the sales boom were the division's full-size models—the Biscayne, Bel Air, Impala and Caprice models. All were totally restyled for 1971, given a long hood/short deck look. New features included slimmer windshield posts, flush-style side glass and flush door handles. The redesigned chassis was longer and featured all-coil suspension. The top model was the Caprice Coupe (right bottom). Its unique concave rear window, luxurious interior and smooth ride made it Chevrolet's most desirable full-size car.

The 1972 GMC MotorHome (left) was designed from the ground up to be one of the most comfortable, efficiently shaped and totally integrated motor homes ever produced. The 26 ft. vehicle rode on a special chassis that was equipped with rear air suspension. A 6.7 liter GMC V-8 drove through the front wheels. Four floor plans were available, sleeping up to six people. With extensive storage space, a complete kitchen and a fully featured bathroom, the GMC MotorHome gave up none of the comforts of home.

Excellent all-around visibility was provided by large tinted windows; the windshield alone measured 32 sq. ft. Exterior and road noise was diminished by a special polyurethane foam barrier covering the entire floor, interior wall and ceiling.

Prefacing the announcement of Opel's Diesel-powered Rekord 2100D was the 1972 Opel Rekordwagen (right). Using a modified Opel GT body with a bubble canopy and a 95 hp, turbocharged, 4 cyl. Diesel, the Rekordwagen broke 20 international Diesel records of up to 10,000 km.

The year 1971 was an important one for GM-Holden's, the year in which the successful HQ series was introduced. The HQ was planned as a car for the 1970's and was an entirely new construction. Safety was one of the major features of its design, and it met or exceeded all Australian safety requirements. The HQ was the most successful Holden ever, with almost half a million built between 1971 and 1974. The 1971 Holden HQ Premier Estate wagon (below) came with a standard 220 cu. in. six.

183

It was a year of milestones for two GM divisions in 1972. Oldsmobile celebrated its 75th anniversary; for Cadillac it was the 70th, and also the second year that the division's annual model production exceeded 270,000 automobiles.

The 1972 Cadillac Eldorado convertible (left top) was one car that helped Cadillac achieve its record. The Eldorado's 500 cu. in. V-8 offered the highest torque on any production car.

The sensational "boattail" styling that debuted on the 1971 Buick Riviera returned for 1972 (right). New for the year, however, were several detail changes made to conform with recent federal safety standards. In order to meet bumper impact standards GM stipulated that all of its 1972 models should be able to withstand a 5 mph direct impact or a 2.5 mph car-to-car impact. This was handled on all Rivieras by an 11% thicker bumper with a strong reinforcing member behind it, allowing for a one-inch deflection. Additional protection came from impact strips on the face of the bumper. Also new for 1972 was a solenoid-actuated throttle stop that eliminated engine run-on by cutting off the carburetor's air supply. The optional Riviera GS package, which originated in 1965, was available yet again in 1973. Its special features included a 260 hp version of the Buick 455 cu. in. V-8, positraction and special GS trim.

The 1972 Hurst/Olds Indianapolis 500 Pace Car (left bottom), the second Oldsmobile in three years to pace the field, was a limited production Cutlass with special performance features. In 1968 Oldsmobile contracted with Hurst Performance Products to install the 455 cu. in. Olds V-8, which was normally used in full-size Oldsmobiles, in the Cutlass. Only 499 Hurst coupes were built in 1972. Overall Olds' sales of more than 750,000 cars put the division into the industry's third place.

GM's extensive testing of the Wankel rotary engine led to the development of an experimental Corvette engine. The mid-engined car, known as the "4-Rotor," boasted a displacement of 585 cu. in. with an output of 350 hp at 7000 rpm. Wind tunnel testing showed a drag coefficient of just 0.325. The 4 Rotor's gullwing doors were equipped with special light-weight safety glass. When rotary engine development ended the car was converted to V-8 power in 1974 and is known today as the "Aerovette" (right).

Pontiac's Grand Am, a 2 door Notchback Hardtop (below) and Chevrolet's Monte Carlo (left) were both cars directed toward a growing market, the personal performance/luxury car. The 1973 Grand Am was available with V-8 engines ranging from 170 to 310 hp. Extensive suspension development led to outstanding handling. Chevrolet's Monte Carlo was more comfort-oriented, with automatic transmission standard; rotating bucket seats were among many options.

Contributing to GM's record sales in 1973 was the Oldsmobile Cutlass S (far right top). Redesigned for the year the Cutlass lineup included Cutlass S, 4-4-2 and Cutlass Supreme models. With sales of over 360,000 Cutlasses Oldsmobile captured third place in sales for the second year in a row. In a Car and Driver Reader's Choice Poll the Cutlass was named the year's best family sedan.

Chevrolet's Vega, introduced in 1971, was an important new entry into the market-place, and brought pleasing proportions to small cars. A GT package offered in late 1971 included such extras as heavy-duty suspension, special instrumentation, wide oval tires and steel sport wheels. This was in addition to a unitized body by Fisher, steel side-guard beams in the doors, front disc brakes and the Vega's aluminum 2.3 liter, OHC, 4 cyl. engine.

The Vega line for 1973 again included a broad range of body styles; notchback, hatchback and panel express models were offered in addition to the Kammback GT wagon (left). Named for aerodynamic researcher Wunibald Kamm, the Vega wagon shared several improvements with the rest of the 1973 Vega lineup. Changes included a new 2 barrel carburetor for the higher output 90 hp engine, a modified cylinder head casting and new 3 and 4 speed transmissions.

Another Chevrolet hatchback was the Nova, a new addition to the Nova line for 1973 (near right top). Its counterbalanced rear hatch opened to a carpeted rear deck that featured as much as 6 ft. of cargo space when the rear seat was folded down. All Novas for 1973 were equipped with flow-through ventilation, improved sound insulation and a 21 gal. fuel tank. Nova sales were 334,371 for the year. (Right bottom) 1973 Chevrolet El Camino. Sharing a redesigned body with the Chevelle, the El Camino was a practical pickup with the comfort of a passenger car. An optional SS package included a 350 or 454 cu. in. V-8, 4 speed transmission and special SS interior trim.

190

Through the 1970's and 1980's Pontiac's Trans Am (below) became one of America's most sought-after performance cars. Carried over for 1974 was the Super Duty 455 cu. in. V-8, 290 hp designed specifically for the Trans Am. The 1974 Opel GT2 (right), a proposed successor to the Opel GT, had a 16% improved drag factor over the production Opel GT. The 1975 Chevrolet Monza (left bottom), derived from the Vega, was an appropriate response to new demands for fuel efficient American automobiles that were sporty as well. The 1974 Vauxhall Ventora (far left top), with a 3.3 liter OHC six, remained a high-performance luxury car with compact dimensions. The 1975 Holden SL/R 5000 (near left top) was the top performance car for the year from GM-Holden's, with a front air dam, rear spoiler, special SL/R decals and a 5 liter V-8 engine.

At 10:12 AM on April 21, 1976 Cadillac built the last American convertible of the 1970's. Inundated with orders for this milestone model Cadillac built 200 "last" white convertibles, keeping the actual last car for its collection. While many thought that convertibles would be gone forever, public tastes would demand their return in the 1980's. (Near right center) 1976 Cadillac Eldorado convertible.

The first small Cadillac ever produced was the 1976 Seville (near right bottom), which offered traditional Cadillac comfort in an international size that coupled good performance with improved fuel economy. Compared with the 1975 full-size Cadillac Coupe de Ville, the Seville was 27 in. shorter, 8 in. narrower, almost identical in height and nearly 1000 lbs. lighter.

The Seville's 5.7 liter V-8 was electronically fuel-injected; sensors at several locations on the engine monitored a wide range of factors to achieve desired performance characteristics. Extensive research and testing of the suspension provided the Seville with a traditionally smooth Cadillac ride while improving handling.

The Chevrolet Chevette, introduced in 1976, quickly established itself as the fuel economy leader of American-built automobiles. Changes for the 1977 Chevette (left) included 13% more horsepower from its 1.4 liter, 4 cyl. engine. An improved air control system and a new camshaft offered improved fuel economy, while similar improvements were also produced in the optional 1.6 liter engine.

Pontiac celebrated its 50th anniversary in 1976 with a Golden Anniversary edition of the Grand Prix (near right top). After the production of the millionth Grand Prix in 1975, the car underwent significant styling and content changes for 1976. Grand Prix sales rose over 150% to a record-breaking level of 228,091 units.

Also breaking records in 1976 was the Oldsmobile Cutlass (far right top). Its high resale value, combined with a wide range of models, helped propel Oldsmobile to a third-place sales slot once again with sales of 514,593 1976 Cutlasses. At the top of the line was the Olds Cutlass Brougham; an in-line 4 liter six was standard and a variety of V-8s were available.

Although produced in limited quantities, Oldsmobile's 1977 Toronado XSR (near left top) helped to push the division's sales for the year over one-million. Among the special features of the XSR were a panoramic rear window and twin, electrically operated glass roof panels that slid inboard and stored over one another in a center T-bar. GM's other front-wheel-drive luxury car was the 1977 Cadillac Eldorado (far left top).

Extensive downsizing of Chevrolet's full-size Impala and Caprice models (left bottom, styling model) led to an overall weight reduction of more than 600 lbs. A 250 cu. in. engine was standard and was EPA-rated at 22 mpg on the highway, 17 mpg in the city. New in 1978 was GMC's RTS (Rapid Transit Series) bus (right). An advanced-design bus for the 1980's the RTS featured a self-contained climate conditioning system and a new, fuel efficient, turbocharged Diesel engine.

Chevrolet's Corvette (below) was restyled for 1977. Extensive interior changes were made as well, with a new console and steering column. Leather seats became standard equipment on all Corvettes.

The celebration of Opel's 80th anniversary in 1978 coincided with the introduction of the sleek new Manta coupe (left). Two OHC sixes were available, with displacements of 2.8 and 3.0 liters, both equipped with electronic fuel injection. Power steering was standard on all Manta models, with a choice of a manual 4 speed or automatic 3 speed transmission.

Chevrolet's 1978 Malibu and Malibu Classic (below) models were responses to the new desires for more efficient and comfortable automobiles. The proportions of the Malibu series were shorter and narrower than 1977 models but offered more interior room and luggage space. Weight reduction played a significant role in the cars' designs. The introduction of the Malibus coincided with the announcement of Chevy's new 3.3 liter V-6. Over 8 in. shorter and some 60 lbs. lighter than the in-line six it replaced, the new V-6 was derived from the successful family of small-block V-8s that originated with the 265 cu. in. V-8 first offered in the 1955 Chevrolet.

Pontiac's popular Trans Am was further enhanced in 1978 by the addition of a Special Edition model (right) finished in gold. Fisher Body T-top roof panels were also included in the package. A new option for the 1978 Trans Am was the W-6 handling package that included special front and rear suspension components, higher effort power steering and 8 in. wide aluminum wheels. Total Trans Am production for the 1978 model year was a record 93,341 units, a 26% increase over the 1977 level. Combining adequate horsepower levels with a modest appetite for fuel was Buick's V-6, reintroduced for the 1974 model year. When Buick was called upon to pace the Indy 500 in 1976, the division created a custom-built turbocharged version of the 231 cu. in. V-6 to power the 1976 Century Pace Car. The following year development work was underway to put the turbo V-6 into production. By the 1978 model year the engine was available in the Regal Sport Coupe and the LeSabre Sport Coupe (below), developing 150 hp.

After growing in size throughout the 1960's and 1970's Buick's fifth generation Riviera returned to its elegant 1963 proportions in 1979. For the first time, however, Buick adopted front-wheel-drive for the Riviera. To achieve the new configuration the engine remained in its longitudinal position, but was moved forward and slightly to the right to provide room for the THM 325 automatic transaxle. Suspension was fully independent, with torsion bars at the front and a rubber-isolated "A" frame lower control arm and coil springs at the rear. Front and rear wheel bearings were lubricated for life.

Two models of the 1979 Riviera were offered; the S-Type and the Luxury Coupe (left). The S-Type was powered by a 3.8 liter turbocharged V-6, while the Luxury Coupe used a 5.7 liter V-8.

Available mid-year was a unique Buick option: a trip monitor digital instrumentation package. The speedometer and fuel gauge had a constant digital readout, and on demand the trip monitor would display the fuel range, time of day, trip odometer, elapsed time, engine temperature and voltage.

For 1979 the Oldsmobile Toronado (right top) shed 900 lbs. and gained a totally new body. The wheelbase was reduced from 122 in. to 114 in.; overall length was 206 in.

The 1979 Eldorado's (right center) lighter weight and new dimensions allowed for improved handling and ride, aided by a 3 ft. reduction in turning radius. Power came from a 5.7 liter V-8, available in gasoline or Diesel versions. The Eldorado retained its front-wheel-drive configuration, but was 20 in. shorter and 8 in. narrower than the 1978 model. A record 67,435 1979 Eldorado coupes were built.

The Opel flagship for 1979 was the Senator CD (right bottom). The lines of the Senator were derived from the Rekord, but overall length of the Senator was increased by 8 in., as emphasized by the small window behind the rear passenger door. The Senator, along with the Opel Manta, used special "Miniblock" double-conical rear springs that allowed 10.5 in. of suspension travel for a smooth ride and confident handling. A 2.8 liter OHC six was standard on the CD model, as was a GM Strasbourg 3 speed automatic transmission.

CHAPTER NINE

CHALLENGE OF THE FUTURE

1980-1984

The direction of the automotive marketplace in the late 1970's and early 1980's proved difficult to predict. Consumer tastes became increasingly varied; while manufacturers worked to reduce the size of automobiles and engines to meet demands for increased fuel efficiency, improved fuel supplies and a stabilization in fuel costs would trigger renewed interest in full-size cars and higher output engines.

Following a downsizing program that trimmed over 900 lbs. from its full-size 1977 car line, GM continued development on a new generation of front-wheel-drive cars. The first of this new series was the "X-body," introduced in 1979 and available in four models—Chevrolet Citation, Oldsmobile Omega, Pontiac Phoenix and Buick Skylark. With either a 2.5 liter four or a 2.8 liter V-6 available, these cars offered fuel economy and performance. Their transverse-engined front-wheel-drive configuration preserved a roomy 5 passenger interior with ample luggage space.

In 1980 GM announced that it was embarking on a massive multi-billion-dollar investment program to re-shape its vehicles, build new assembly plants and modernize and/or expand existing manufacturing facilities. The first products to emerge from this new commitment were the subcompact Chevrolet Cavalier, Pontiac J2000 and Cadillac Cimarron, offered initially in 1981. Designed from the ground up to meet import competition head-to-head, the new cars emulated the "X-body" with spacious interior and compact exterior dimensions, and came with a wide range of standard equipment. Notchback, hatchback, sedan and wagon versions were available from Pontiac and Chevrolet; the Cadillac Cimarron was offered only as a 4 door sedan. Versions of the new compact from Buick (the Skyhawk) and Oldsmobile (the Firenza) were available later in 1981.

For 1982 30% of GM's car lines were brand new. Leading the pack were the mid-size front-wheel-drive Chevrolet Celebrity, Pontiac 6000, Oldsmobile Ciera and Buick Century. With lines as smooth to the eye as they were to the airstream, these cars attracted full-size car buyers because of their excellent fuel efficiency and ample interior room.

Debuting in 1982 were the totally redesigned Pontiac Firebird and Chevrolet Camaro. Both cars were reborn as striking wedges that presented a "clean" face to the wind, and were available with 4, 6, or 8 cyl. engines.

Overseas, Opel introduced its first front-wheel-drive car, the 1980 Kadett D. A totally new 1.3 liter OHC four was Opel's first engine to use a cross-flow cylinder head, which was also the first cylinder head to be made of aluminum. The Kadett, developed in collaboration with Vauxhall, would bow in England the same year as the Vauxhall Astra.

In 1981 GM of Canada produced its fourteen-millionth vehicle. Later in that year GM-Holden's began construction of a new 4 cyl. engine facility to build power-plants for its new 1982 Camira.

On October 1, 1982 GM officially opened its World of Motion exhibit in the Epcot Center at Walt Disney World in Florida. Entertaining and informative the World of Motion was created in the tradition of GM's famed Futurama and Highways and Horizons exhibits at the New York World's Fair in 1964 and 1939.

With economic recovery underway by mid 1983, sales began to rebound as consumers opted for GM cars that combined state-of-the-art engineering and aerodynamic technology with attractive styling. Leading the way into GM's next 75 years are the sophisticated 1984 Chevrolet Corvette and Pontiac Fiero 2M4, GM's first mid-engined car.

The 1980 front-wheel drive Chevrolet Citation (far right top) was offered in 2 or 4 door hatchback models. Oldsmobile's version of the front-wheel-drive compact was the Omega (near right top), available in 2 and 4 door notchback models.

Vauxhall introduced its first front-wheel-drive car in 1980. The Astra (above) was wedge-shaped, with a deep front air dam, a high tail and flowing body lines.

Chevrolet's light-duty pickups in 1981 (below), were lighter, leaner, more fuel-efficient and sported all-new aerodynamically designed sheet metal from the cowl forward.

Sharing the spotlight with the 1982 Chevrolet Cavalier was the Pontiac J2000 (above top). Like its Chevrolet cousin, the J2000 featured a transverse-mounted, 1.8 liter, 4 cyl. engine, McPherson strut front suspension and ample room for 4 passengers and their luggage.

The hot Chevrolet Camaro Z-28 (right bottom) was given functional hood air intakes and fender ports for 1980. The standard powertrain for the Z-28 was a 5.7 liter V-8 coupled with a 4 speed manual transmission.

The 1980 Holden Commodore SL/E (left) was a compact but potent luxury sedan that competed with Europe's finest touring cars. It was designed specifically for the Australian environment. Inside, the SL/E featured full instrumentation, including a trip computer that offered information on 7 different areas such as average speed and fuel consumption.

The 1980 Cadillac Seville was a unique combination of contemporary and classic styling themes. The front end was similar to that of the original 1976 Seville, while the rear area harkened back to the 1930's "bustleback" look. Also new was front-wheel-drive, making the car the first sedan to combine front-wheel-drive, 4 wheel independent suspension, 4 wheel disc brakes, electronic leveling control, a standard V-8 Diesel and cruise control. Gasoline-engined Sevilles used a 6 liter Cadillac-built V-8 with digital electronic fuel injection (EFI).

The 1980 Seville Elegante (below) was the ultimate Seville, offering three exclusive two-tone paint combinations.

Buick's popular Regal was redesigned for 1981 and featured several mechanical improvements. Three models of the Regal were available; a base Regal, the Sport Coupe and the Regal Limited (right), which emphasized luxury.
New mechanical features on the 1981 Regals included Computer Command Control, which was introduced in California in 1978 on GM cars with gasoline engines, and became standard on all GM gasoline-engined cars in the 1981 model year. The heart of the system was an on-board computer that continuously monitored and adjusted air/fuel ratio and spark timing to control exhaust emissions and improve fuel economy.
A sporty version of Chevrolet's Cavalier series was the Type 10 (below). Based on the Cavalier CL the Type 10 was available with Chevrolet's renowned F41 suspension package that featured front and rear sway bars, stiffer springs and shock valving and solid rubber bushings for the rear suspension.

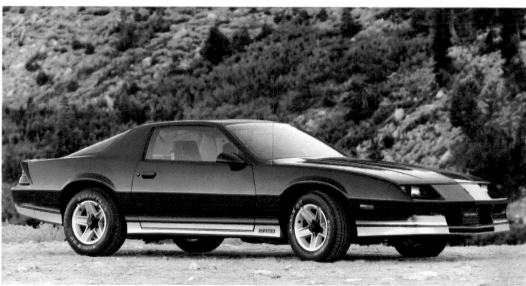

Aerodynamics assumed an even greater role in automotive design through the 1980's. Few cars have undergone as extensive aerodynamic development as the 1982 Chevrolet Celebrity (left). Nine series of wind tunnel tests showed that the car's flush-mounted windshield glass, integrated side mirrors, front spoiler and rear deck spoiler lip combined to give it a low drag factor.

In addition to its functional good looks the Celebrity featured a list of standard equipment, including automatic transmission, power steering and brakes, fiberglass-belted radial tires and side window defoggers. Three engines were available: a 2.5 liter four, a 2.8 liter V-6 and a 4.3 liter V-6 Diesel. GM's continuing aerodynamic research is shown in Opel's 1982 Tech I (above), a project car based on the front-wheel-drive production Kadett D. Combining 4 door practicality with a sleek appearance, the Tech I featured a low profile frontal area with "flow favorable" side panels enhanced by flush-mounted window glass.

A new generation of fuel-efficient performance cars, with sporty and aerodynamic styling, was typified by the 1982 Chevrolet Camaro Z-28 (right top) and Pontiac Firebird Trans Am (right bottom). Extensive redesigning of both cars resulted in a wind-cheating shape, while suspension development yielded new levels of sports car handling.

GM-Holden's took the front-wheel-drive compact car and tailored it for Australian driving conditions. The Holden Camira, along with its American and European cousins, benefited from advanced technology in several areas. Using a process known as Finite Element Analysis, a computer model of the car was tested to see which areas of the body were under stress and adjusted the type of materials used in the body structure accordingly. The Camira's "Camtech 4" 4 cyl. OHC engine featured an "Engine Management Module" that adjusted idle speed and monitored exhaust emissions. The top Camira for 1982 was the SL/E (left bottom).

In Europe GM's new subcompact car program combined optimal efficiency in a small package. The first car to debut in the series was the 1982 Opel Corsa, built at GM's new Spanish assembly plant near Zaragoza. The Corsa, the smallest car ever built by GM, was similar in size to other European "microminis," but had the largest amount of interior room. Two versions of the Corsa were available initially, a hatchback (left top) and a notchback. The front-wheel-drive Corsa's suspension used McPherson struts at the front and an Opel designed "compound crank" system at the rear. Engines ranged from a 1.0 liter OHV four to a 1.3 liter OHC four.

GM's World of Motion exhibit in the Epcot Center at Walt Disney World in Florida features a sound-equipped chair ride—a revolutionary idea when GM introduced it at the New York World's Fair in 1939—and a special Transcenter area that highlights GM's futuristic research and development. In a quarter-hour on the Disney-developed ride, visitors span the ages that people have spent seeking a better means of moving from here to there. The 24 animated dioramas show how transportation has influenced the evolution of society. The Transcenter area of the exhibit features entertaining and informative illustrations of GM's pathfinder role in auto industry research, engineering, design and manufacturing. Transcenter also looks ahead. In a rare view of a design studio, visitors see the "Aero 2000" (right top), a 4 seater with estimated fuel economy of 71 mpg, and how it was created. Nearby the "Lean Machine" (right bottom), a 1 passenger motorcycle-type commuter vehicle capable of 60 mph in 7 sec., appears on film and in model form.

207

Throughout the late 1970's the American automotive marketplace proved to be as difficult to predict as the weather. Although the "last" American convertible, a Cadillac Eldorado, rolled off the line in April 1976, the buying public of the early 1980's was eager for ragtops once again. Buick was the first GM division to respond to this new taste, offering a convertible version of the 1983 Riviera. Chevrolet soon followed with an open-air version of its Cavalier (left top), and Pontiac offered its 2000 Sunbird.

As gasoline prices stabilized and adequate fuel supplies seemed assured, consumers renewed their interest in performance along with fuel efficiency. One example of GM's reply to this interest is Pontiac's 1983 sporty 6000 STE (right top). Aimed squarely at the European sports car enthusiast the 6000 STE features strong performance combined with European-class handling. Power for the 6000 STE comes from a high output V-6 engine, producing 135 hp.

The front-wheel-drive 6000 STE has McPherson struts at the front and a beam axle with trailing arms and an integral roll bar at the rear. The 6000 STE also has a standard self-leveling rear suspension system.

Sharing the front-wheel-drive mid-size design with other GM divisions is the 1983 Oldsmobile Cutlass Ciera (left bottom). The V-6 Diesel used in the mid-size cars was developed by Oldsmobile and represents extensive research and advancement in passenger car Diesel engines. The use of hydraulic lifters with roller bearings eliminates premature camshaft wear, while a special inertia-weight flywheel smooths out the Diesel's power pulses.

Extra insulation and sound-deadening material reduce the noise usually associated with Diesel engines.

Buick's Electra for 1983 (right bottom) combines luxury with good fuel economy, thanks to an improved standard 4.1 liter, 4 barrel, V-6 engine and automatic transmission with overdrive.

Bedford's latest, the 1983 TM 4400 (left), is of the series that took Bedford from building medium-sized trucks into the long haul, heavy-duty European class. Based on a modular design offering two widths with an interchange of panels between widths, the new TM 4400 has a capacity of 44 tons and Diesel power of 387 bhp net.

(Right top) Vauxhall's front-wheel-drive 1983 Cavalier GLS 4 door. The power output is a very healthy 90 bhp at 5800 rpm, putting it in the top of the 1.6 liter class. New for 1983 is a 5 speed overdrive transmission.

Cadillac's sporty 1983 Eldorado Touring Coupe (above) features the division's new, HT 4100 aluminum-block, 4.1 liter V-8.

(Right bottom) one of the world's largest load carrying dump trucks, the Titan 33-15C was built by the Diesel Division of GM of Canada Ltd., London, Ontario in 1971 for open-pit mining. Powered by a 1600 hp Detroit Diesel that drives a generator powering two inboard electric motors geared directly to the rear wheels, this massive truck is a railless road locomotive capable of carrying 170 tons of rock-ore. To stop such rolling tonnage sophisticated brakes similar to those of a freight locomotive were developed. A three times larger dump truck, the Titan 19, the first of a new generation, is presently operating in Canada's British Columbia mines.

(Left) GMC's 1983 Aero Astro, an aerodynamic, fuel-efficient, heavy-duty tractor featuring a new front end and bumper design with air dam smoothing the air up and to the sides. On the cab's roof is a full width GM-developed Dragfoiler with accordian fold sides that adjust to different angles to accommodate varying trailer heights and shapes to further reduce air turbulence. Large fiberglass panels are positioned between the cab and the trailer, further smoothing the vehicle's air flow and minimizing cross-wind effects.

Sleeper models are optional and a full range of Detroit Diesels is available to meet a wide variety of power requirements.

(Near right top) One of the 47 new all-electric powered locomotives delivered by Electro-Motive Division to Amtrak for its high speed passenger trains in the Northeast Corridor. Each unit generates an equivalent of 7000 hp in an electric Diesel.

GM's Electro-Motive Division over the past 40 years has compiled an outstanding record of engine design; many of the more than 50,000 medium speed, 2 cycle Diesel engines produced are still in service. (Far right top) EMD's latest locomotive, the GP 50, a turbocharged 16 cyl. developing 3500 hp for traction at 950 rpm and incorporating Super Series Adhesion Control, which improves wheel adhesion 33%. There is a 200 rpm low idle system for fuel efficiency, the first time 3500 hp has been available on a four-axle locomotive.

Following the lead of the amazingly successful S-10 compact pickup series, Chevrolet introduced an S-10 four-wheel-drive Blazer for 1983 (right bottom), while GMC offered the Jimmy. With independent front suspension, front bucket seats, 8.8 in. ground clearance and a high/low range transmission, the new Blazer is at home on highway or hillside. A vacuum-operated front transfer case allows shifting into four-wheel-drive at any speed. The new Blazer is 15.3 in. shorter and 14.8 in. narrower than its predecessor, but has slightly more load space. Power is supplied by 2.0 liter (49 states) and 1.9 liter (California) 4 cyl. engines; an optional 2.8 liter V-6 is available in all 50 states.

BUILDING ON 75 YEARS OF EXCELLENCE

During GM's first 75 years over 235 million automobiles and commercial vehicles were produced; over half the automobiles built in the entire world have carried the GM imprint, offering testimony to GM's unparalleled achievement. Continual improvement and refinement in the technology of mass production provide "every purse, purpose and person" an automobile for pleasure or business. On the basis of any evaluation this distinctive contribution constitutes an economical, social and technological revolution surpassing that of the invention of the automobile itself.

The success of GM is based on considerably more than numbers, overwhelming and impressive as they may be. Beginning with its founding in 1908, the hallmark of GM's success has been the ability of the corporation and its people to respond effectively to new circumstances. Witness the calendar of three-quarters of a century of fluctuating business cycles, a devastating world-wide Depression, four destructive and turbulent wars, unceasing competition on all sides at home and abroad and increased government regulations—all this well mixed into times of high prosperity and peace.

Twenty-five years hence, when GM celebrates its centennial, the challenges it faces today, like those of our nation, will have slipped into history as a continuous testimony to the character of our people to excel in every challenge. Then, as now, there will be challenges, successes to honor and to take pride in. This has been the history of our country, the history of GM.

Over 235 million vehicles from GM, its 75 years of building on excellence, speak eloquently for GM's contribution to the American way of life.

(Left) 1984 Pontiac Fiero 2M4. (Right) 1984 Chevrolet Corvette.

CALENDAR

General Motors has produced over 235 million vehicles worldwide since its incorporation in 1908. The following figures summarize calendar year production of cars, trucks, commercial vehicles, buses and coaches over the past 75 years by GM's North American operations and major overseas subsidiaries. Yearly production figures for trucks are combined with those of passenger cars where applicable. Not included here are production totals of various overseas associated companies.

Between 1910 and 1922 GM produced cars with marques other than Chevrolet, Oakland, Oldsmobile, Buick and Cadillac. These marques included Cartercar, Elmore, Marquette, Randolph, Welch, Scripps-Booth and Sheridan. Their combined production totalled 44,609 units.

While there may be slight discrepancies in the totals because of incomplete early records, every effort has been taken to make the production figures as accurate as possible.

1908	
Buick	8,820
Oldsmobile	1,055
TOTAL	9,875

1909	
Buick	14,606
Cadillac	7,868
Oakland	—
Oldsmobile	1,690
TOTAL	24,164

1910	
Buick	20,758
Cadillac	10,039
Oakland	4,049
Oldsmobile	1,425
TOTAL	36,271

1911	
Buick	18,844
Cadillac	10,071
GM Truck	293
Oakland	3,386
Oldsmobile	1,271
TOTAL	33,865

1912	
Buick	26,796
Cadillac	12,708
GM Truck	158
Oakland	5,838
Oldsmobile	1,155
TOTAL	46,655

1913	
Buick	29,722

From 1916 to 1927 GM owned a 10 story structure at 224 West 57th Street, New York City. In 1927 the corporation moved to a 25 story building at 1775 Broadway, shown at left. GM retained this New York City address until 1968.

Cadillac	17,284
GM Truck	601
Oakland	7,030
Oldsmobile	1,175
TOTAL	**55,812**

1914

Buick	42,803
Cadillac	7,818
GM Truck	708
Oakland	6,105
Oldsmobile	2,254
TOTAL	**59,688**

1915

Buick	60,662
Cadillac	20,404
GM Truck	1,408
Oakland	11,952
Oldsmobile	7,696
TOTAL	**102,122**

1916

Buick	90,925
Cadillac	16,323
GM Truck	2,999
Oakland	25,675
Oldsmobile	10,263
TOTAL	**146,185**

1917

Buick	122,262
Cadillac	19,725
GM Truck	5,885
Oakland	33,171
Oldsmobile	22,027
TOTAL	**203,070**

1918

Buick	81,413
Cadillac	12,329
Chevrolet	81,823
GM Truck	8,999
GM of Canada	20,160
Oakland	27,757
Oldsmobile	18,871
TOTAL	**251,352**

1919

Buick	115,401
Cadillac	19,851
Chevrolet	117,840
GM Truck	7,730
GM of Canada	24,085
Oakland	52,124
Oldsmobile	41,127
TOTAL	**378,158**

1920

Buick	112,249
Cadillac	19,628
Chevrolet	134,794
GM Truck	5,327
GM of Canada	23,052
Oakland	37,141
Oldsmobile	35,412
TOTAL	**367,603**

1921

Buick	82,930
Cadillac	11,273
Chevrolet	67,999
GM Truck	2,915
GM of Canada	15,544
Oakland	11,197
Oldsmobile	17,743
TOTAL	**209,601**

1922

Buick	123,152
Cadillac	22,500
Chevrolet	227,755
GM Truck	5,534
GM of Canada	37,438
Oakland	20,941
Oldsmobile	18,393
TOTAL	**455,713**

1923

Buick	201,572
Cadillac	21,756
Chevrolet	457,608
GM Truck	7,429
GM of Canada	43,923
Oakland	36,566
Oldsmobile	34,811
TOTAL	**803,665**

1924

Buick	156,627
Cadillac	17,748
Chevrolet	287,150
GM Truck	5,508
GM of Canada	34,507
Oakland	35,792
Oldsmobile	44,309
TOTAL	**581,641**

1925

Buick	192,100
Cadillac	22,197
Chevrolet	443,569
* GM Truck	2,468
GM of Canada	44,829
Oakland	43,018
Oldsmobile	43,386
Vauxhall	1,398
TOTAL	**792,965**

1926

Buick	266,753
Cadillac	28,402
Chevrolet	693,386
GM of Canada	56,683
Oakland-Pontiac	132,971
Oldsmobile	57,878
Vauxhall	1,527
TOTAL	**1,237,600**

1927

Buick	255,160
Cadillac-LaSalle	35,106
Chevrolet	940,140
GM of Canada	91,268
Oakland-Pontiac	183,663
Oldsmobile	54,245
Vauxhall	751
TOTAL	**1,560,333**

1928

Buick	221,758
Cadillac-LaSalle	41,375
Chevrolet	1,123,995
GM of Canada	102,424
Oakland-Pontiac	243,718
Oldsmobile	86,593
Vauxhall	2,560
TOTAL	**1,822,423**

1929

Buick	196,104
Cadillac-LaSalle	36,666
Chevrolet	1,242,260
GM of Canada	104,198
Oakland-Pontiac	216,826
Oldsmobile-Viking	103,973
Vauxhall	1,668
TOTAL	**1,901,695**

1930

Buick-Marquette	119,265
Cadillac-LaSalle	22,559
Chevrolet	824,470
GM of Canada	55,379
Oakland-Pontiac	82,259
Oldsmobile-Viking	50,326
Vauxhall	1,277
TOTAL	**1,155,535**

1931

Bedford	11,487
Buick	87,633
Cadillac-LaSalle	15,278
Chevrolet	759,839
GM of Canada	32,791
Oakland-Pontiac	90,029
Oldsmobile	48,777
Opel	26,689
Vauxhall	3,492
TOTAL	**1,076,015**

1932

Bedford	10,529
Buick	42,306
Cadillac-LaSalle	7,975
Chevrolet	380,607
GM of Canada	19,565
Oldsmobile	17,502
Opel	20,982
Pontiac	42,633
Vauxhall	2,136
TOTAL	**544,235**

1933

Bedford	15,173
Buick	40,620
Cadillac-LaSalle	5,860
Chevrolet	609,996

217

*U.S. production figures for GM Truck are not available from 1926 to the early 1940's and the formation of GMC Truck & Coach Division. During this period GM Truck was part of Yellow Truck and Coach Manufacturing Company, a holding company whose operations were not consolidated in the accounts of GM.

GM of Canada	21,887
Oldsmobile	36,072
Opel	39,193
Pontiac	85,666
Vauxhall	9,949
TOTAL	**864,416**

1934

Bedford	17,823
Buick	78,757
Cadillac-LaSalle	12,226
Chevrolet	835,909
GM of Canada	43,075
Oldsmobile	82,150
Opel	72,061
Pontiac	80,195
Vauxhall	20,227
TOTAL	**1,242,423**

1935

Bedford	23,741
Buick	107,611
Cadillac-LaSalle	23,191
Chevrolet	1,022,180
GM of Canada	60,609
Oldsmobile	182,491
Opel	102,293
Pontiac	175,268
Vauxhall	22,118
TOTAL	**1,719,502**

1936

Bedford	26,210
Buick	179,533
Cadillac-LaSalle	28,447
Chevrolet	1,227,062
GM of Canada	61,830
Oldsmobile	187,150
Opel	120,852
Pontiac	178,496
Vauxhall	17,640
TOTAL	**2,027,220**

1937

Bedford	31,783
Buick	227,038
Cadillac-LaSalle	45,223
Chevrolet	1,128,849
GM of Canada	81,742
Oldsmobile	212,331
Opel	130,267
Pontiac	235,322
Vauxhall	30,616
TOTAL	**2,123,171**

1938

Bedford	27,474
Buick	173,905
Cadillac-LaSalle	27,613
Chevrolet	653,338
GM of Canada	55,994
Oldsmobile	93,706
Opel	140,580
Pontiac	95,128
Vauxhall	32,224
TOTAL	**1,299,962**

1939

Bedford	18,185
Buick	231,219
Cadillac-LaSalle	38,520
Chevrolet	892,092
GM of Canada	53,928
Oldsmobile	158,560
Opel	—
Pontiac	170,698
Vauxhall	34,367
TOTAL	**1,597,569**

1940

Bedford	54,696
Buick	310,995
Cadillac-LaSalle	40,245
Chevrolet	1,141,867
GMC	61,660
GM of Canada	74,838
Oldsmobile	215,028
Opel	—
Pontiac	249,303
Vauxhall	18,543
TOTAL	**2,167,175**

1941

Bedford	39,873
Buick	316,251
Cadillac	59,572
Chevrolet	1,250,281
GMC	113,803
GM of Canada	107,964
Oldsmobile	230,703
Opel	—
Pontiac	282,087
Vauxhall	—
TOTAL	**2,400,534**

1942

Bedford	46,761
Buick	16,601
Cadillac	2,873
Chevrolet	164,470
GMC	150,506
GM of Canada	82,970
Oldsmobile	12,230
Opel	—
Pontiac	15,404
Vauxhall	—
TOTAL	**491,815**

1943

Bedford	48,648
Buick	—
Cadillac	—
Chevrolet	60,429
GMC	136,461
GM of Canada	61,747
Oldsmobile	—
Opel	—
Pontiac	—
Vauxhall	—
TOTAL	**307,285**

1944

Bedford	34,124
Buick	—
Cadillac	—
Chevrolet	71,269
GMC	152,992
GM of Canada	53,395
Oldsmobile	—
Opel	—
Pontiac	—
Vauxhall	—
TOTAL	**311,780**

1945

Bedford	38,773
Buick	2,482
Cadillac	1,142
Chevrolet	107,411
GMC	113,126
GM of Canada	46,044
Oldsmobile	3,498
Opel	—
Pontiac	5,606
Vauxhall	—
TOTAL	**318,082**

1946

Bedford	33,809
Buick	156,080
Cadillac	28,444
Chevrolet	667,260
GMC	36,289
GM of Canada	51,772
Oldsmobile	114,674
Opel	839
Pontiac	131,538
Vauxhall	19,713
TOTAL	**1,240,418**

1947

Bedford	31,077
Buick	267,830
Cadillac	59,436
Chevrolet	1,031,338
GMC	67,424
GM of Canada	85,360
Oldsmobile	191,454
Opel	3,239
Pontiac	223,015
Vauxhall	30,376
TOTAL	**1,990,549**

1948

Bedford	35,522
Buick	275,503
Cadillac	66,209
Chevrolet	1,165,680
GMC	98,039
GM of Canada	93,742
* Holden	163
Oldsmobile	194,755
Opel	13,091
Pontiac	253,469
Vauxhall	38,062
TOTAL	**2,234,235**

1949

Bedford	38,115
Buick	398,482
Cadillac	81,545
Chevrolet	1,493,501
GMC	86,016
GM of Canada	92,330
Holden	7,724
Oldsmobile	282,885
Opel	39,564
Pontiac	336,445
Vauxhall	45,032
TOTAL	**2,901,639**

1950

Bedford	40,591
Buick	552,827
Cadillac	110,535
Chevrolet	2,015,158

*From 1924 until 1949 Holden produced 351,132 bodies for GM.

GMC		112,779
GM of Canada		160,164
Holden		20,190
Oldsmobile		396,757
Opel		72,746
Pontiac		469,813
Vauxhall		47,652
	TOTAL	3,999,212

1951

Bedford		42,677
Buick		404,695
Cadillac		103,266
Chevrolet		1,544,216
GMC		131,814
GM of Canada		187,465
Holden		25,249
Oldsmobile		285,634
Opel		76,955
Pontiac		345,617
Vauxhall		34,922
	TOTAL	3,182,510

1952

Bedford		44,178
Buick		321,048
Cadillac		96,850
Chevrolet		1,210,100
GMC		121,884
GM of Canada		200,310
Holden		31,918
Oldsmobile		228,452
Opel		87,934
Pontiac		278,140
Vauxhall		35,979
	TOTAL	2,656,793

1953

Bedford		48,613
Buick		485,353
Cadillac		103,538
Chevrolet		1,839,132
GMC		116,654
GM of Canada		219,967
Holden		44,201
Oldsmobile		319,414
Opel		105,792
Pontiac		415,335
Vauxhall		61,545
	TOTAL	3,759,544

1954

Bedford		57,896
Buick		531,463
Cadillac		123,746
Chevrolet		1,739,880
GMC		79,019
GM of Canada		153,476
Holden		54,793
Oldsmobile		433,810
Opel		167,650
Pontiac		370,887
Vauxhall		72,515
	TOTAL	3,785,135

1955

Bedford		67,698
Buick		781,296
Cadillac		153,334
Chevrolet		2,223,360
GMC		107,647
GM of Canada		158,320
Holden		63,908
Oldsmobile		643,459
Opel		185,340
Pontiac		581,860
Vauxhall		75,323
	TOTAL	5,041,545

1956

Bedford		63,276
Buick		535,364
Cadillac		140,873
Chevrolet		1,974,528
GMC		94,397
GM of Canada		188,808
Holden		68,883
Oldsmobile		432,903
Opel		207,010
Pontiac		332,268
Vauxhall		64,595
	TOTAL	4,102,905

1957

Bedford		58,483
Buick		407,271
Cadillac		153,236
Chevrolet		1,874,289
GMC		72,783
GM of Canada		181,967
Holden		95,147
Oldsmobile		390,091
Opel		228,903
Pontiac		343,298
Vauxhall		88,493
	TOTAL	3,893,961

1958

Bedford		55,439
Buick		257,124
Cadillac		125,501
Chevrolet		1,534,575
GMC		64,173
GM of Canada		185,731
Holden		110,241
Oldsmobile		310,795
Opel		315,945
Pontiac		219,823
Vauxhall		119,177
	TOTAL	3,298,524

1959

Bedford		88,720
Buick		232,579
Cadillac		138,527
Chevrolet		1,755,082
GMC		77,529
GM do Brasil		16,300
GM of Canada		179,583
Holden		116,348
Oldsmobile		366,305
Opel		331,520
Pontiac		388,856
Vauxhall		157,365
	TOTAL	3,848,714

1960

Bedford		106,284
Buick		307,804
Cadillac		158,941
Chevrolet		2,267,635
GMC		104,327
GM do Brasil		18,176
GM of Canada		209,405
Holden		139,619
Oldsmobile		402,612
Opel		370,073
Pontiac		450,206
Vauxhall		145,742
	TOTAL	4,680,824

1961

Bedford		94,595
Buick		291,285
Cadillac		148,298
Chevrolet		1,947,479
GMC		74,996
GM do Brasil		13,689
GM of Canada		196,244
Holden		112,377
Oldsmobile		321,838
Opel		382,738
Pontiac		360,336
Vauxhall		85,370
	TOTAL	4,029,245

1962

Bedford		76,661
Buick		415,892
Cadillac		158,528
Chevrolet		2,558,349
GMC		89,789
GM do Brasil		18,980
GM of Canada		267,411
Holden		133,274
Oldsmobile		458,359
Opel		379,311
Pontiac		547,350
Vauxhall		144,144
	TOTAL	5,248,048

1963

Bedford		84,798
Buick		479,399
Cadillac		164,735
Chevrolet		2,786,473
GMC		101,234
GM Argentina		3,847
GM do Brasil		12,174
GM of Canada		308,518
Holden		166,274
Oldsmobile		504,555
Opel		570,293
Pontiac		625,268
Vauxhall		164,987
	TOTAL	5,972,555

1964

Bedford		106,672
Buick		482,731
Cadillac		154,623
Chevrolet		2,638,509
GMC		110,521
GM Argentina		19,109
GM do Brasil		13,864
GM of Canada		293,842
Holden		170,919
Oldsmobile		510,931
Opel		688,575
Pontiac		693,634
Vauxhall		246,896
	TOTAL	6,130,826

1965

Bedford		113,825
Buick		653,838
Cadillac		196,595
Chevrolet		3,207,199
GMC		136,705
GM Argentina		25,212
GM do Brasil		10,981
GM of Canada		420,131
GM de Mexico		9,210
GM South African		692
Holden		165,310
Oldsmobile		650,801
Opel		631,137

Pontiac 860,652
Vauxhall 225,088

TOTAL 7,307,376

1966

Bedford 101,898
Buick 580,421
Cadillac 205,001
Chevrolet 2,824,146
GMC 127,294
GM Argentina 21,596
GM do Brasil 15,951
GM of Canada 355,993
GM de Mexico 22,309
GM South African 25,120
Holden 140,859
Oldsmobile 594,069
Opel 662,348
Pontiac 866,385
Vauxhall 164,185

TOTAL 6,707,575

1967

Bedford 89,296
Buick 573,866
Cadillac 213,161
Chevrolet 2,470,330
GMC 130,659
GM Argentina 22,062
GM do Brasil 17,158
GM of Canada 386,241
GM de Mexico 23,693
GM South African 29,182
Holden 147,758
Oldsmobile 552,997
Opel 549,281
Pontiac 857,171
Vauxhall 196,882

TOTAL 6,259,737

1968

Bedford 97,925
Buick 652,049
Cadillac 210,904
Chevrolet 2,829,060

GMC 148,479
GM Argentina 22,361
GM do Brasil 24,987
GM of Canada 424,633
GM de Mexico 27,253
GM South African 23,077
Holden 166,941
Oldsmobile 637,779
Opel 656,718
Pontiac 943,253
Vauxhall 247,034

TOTAL 7,112,453

1969

Bedford 101,821
Buick 713,832
Cadillac 266,798
Chevrolet 2,684,057
GMC 150,180
GM Argentina 30,433
GM do Brasil 52,805
GM of Canada 498,382
GM de Mexico 27,351
GM South African 28,658
Holden 179,258
Oldsmobile 668,399
Opel 801,205
Pontiac 772,104
Vauxhall 169,456

TOTAL 7,144,739

1970

Bedford 101,660
Buick 459,931
Cadillac 152,859
Chevrolet 1,997,215
GMC 121,833
GM Argentina 32,788
GM do Brasil 70,308
GM of Canada 291,272
GM de Mexico 26,043
GM South African 31,542
Holden 186,342
Oldsmobile 439,632
Opel 820,852
Pontiac 422,212

Vauxhall 178,089

TOTAL 5,332,578

1971

Bedford 126,394
Buick 751,885
Cadillac 276,560
Chevrolet 3,060,233
GMC 171,955
GM Argentina 31,953
GM do Brasil 83,297
GM of Canada 507,461
GM de Mexico 32,597
GM South African 15,522
Holden 191,670
Oldsmobile 775,191
Opel 838,718
Pontiac 728,615
Vauxhall 199,092

TOTAL 7,791,143

1972

Bedford 91,053
Buick 688,557
Cadillac 277,251
Chevrolet 3,070,543
GMC 195,332
GM Argentina 27,283
GM do Brasil 104,498
GM of Canada 459,263
GM de Mexico 29,883
GM South African 22,706
Holden 185,935
Oldsmobile 807,194
Opel 877,963
Pontiac 702,571
Vauxhall 183,957

TOTAL 7,723,989

1973

Bedford 107,257
Buick 826,206
Cadillac 307,698
Chevrolet 3,347,984

GMC 247,825
GM Argentina 29,825
GM do Brasil 140,570
GM of Canada 580,984
GM de Mexico 37,123
GM South African 37,096
Holden 200,888
Oldsmobile 918,119
Opel 874,355
Pontiac 866,598
Vauxhall 139,812

TOTAL 8,662,340

1974

Bedford 112,151
Buick 400,262
Cadillac 230,649
Chevrolet 2,771,716
GMC 219,316
GM Argentina 27,731
GM do Brasil 182,319
GM of Canada 646,056
GM de Mexico 38,157
GM South African 31,249
Holden 190,039
Oldsmobile 548,658
Opel 583,645
Pontiac 502,083
Vauxhall 136,903

TOTAL 6,620,934

1975

Bedford 91,540
Buick 535,820
Cadillac 278,404
Chevrolet 2,460,315
GMC 197,008
GM Argentina 24,102
GM do Brasil 173,948
GM of Canada 596,545
GM de Mexico 39,006
GM South African 31,303
Holden 133,679
Oldsmobile 654,342
Opel 657,539
Pontiac 523,469

Vauxhall 98,621

TOTAL 6,495,641

1976

Bedford 86,269
Buick 817,669
Cadillac 312,845
Chevrolet 3,060,537
GMC 293,997
GM Argentina 16,555
GM do Brasil 181,144
GM of Canada 713,337
GM de Mexico 37,624
GM South African 23,484
Holden 131,929
Oldsmobile 964,425
Opel 921,696
Pontiac 784,631
Vauxhall 109,031

TOTAL 8,455,173

1977

Bedford 91,747
Buick 801,202
Cadillac 369,254
Chevrolet 3,255,572
GMC 321,009
GM Argentina 20,921
GM do Brasil 155,564
GM of Canada 779,298
GM de Mexico 30,812
GM South African 16,854
Holden 113,286
Oldsmobile 1,079,841
Opel 925,167
Pontiac 875,957
Vauxhall 95,658

TOTAL 8,932,142

1978

Bedford 117,443
Buick 810,324
Cadillac 350,761
Chevrolet 3,562,205
GMC 375,000

GM Argentina	6,808
GM do Brasil	194,808
GM of Canada	856,102
GM de Mexico	49,424
GM South African	21,258
Holden	127,894
Oldsmobile	910,249
Opel	956,455
Pontiac	867,010
Vauxhall	91,654
TOTAL	9,297,395

1979

Bedford	87,650
Buick	787,149
Cadillac	345,831
Chevrolet	3,251,263
GMC	337,381
GM do Brasil	207,730
GM of Canada	847,736
GM de Mexico	54,418
GM South African	12,138
Holden	141,446
Oldsmobile	1,008,246
Opel	968,466
Pontiac	714,467
Vauxhall	62,086
TOTAL	8,826,007

1980

Bedford	89,829
Buick	783,575
Cadillac	203,991
Chevrolet	2,252,374
GMC	173,702
GM do Brasil	231,557
GM of Canada	767,805
GM de Mexico	38,774
GM South African	11,765
Holden	93,446
Oldsmobile	783,225
Opel	792,800
Pontiac	556,429
Vauxhall	58,687
TOTAL	6,837,959

1981

Bedford	42,492
Buick	839,960
Cadillac	259,135
Chevrolet	1,995,746
GMC	175,208
GM do Brasil	144,139
GM of Canada	757,126
GM de Mexico	67,236
GM South African	55,149
Holden	126,625
Oldsmobile	838,333
Opel	758,786
Other overseas plants	127,103
Pontiac	519,292
Vauxhall	70,198
TOTAL	6,776,528

1982

Bedford	45,357
Buick	751,338
Cadillac	246,602
Chevrolet	1,676,878
GMC	224,306
GM do Brasil	172,571
GM of Canada	561,696
GM de Mexico	44,479
GM South African	38,505
Holden	126,717
Oldsmobile	759,631
Opel	910,356
Other overseas plants	123,069
Pontiac	411,324
Vauxhall	116,048
TOTAL	6,208,877

Pictured at right is GM's New York City location since 1968, at 767 Fifth Avenue. GM's Detroit headquarters at 3044 West Grand Boulevard, pictured on the title page, was completed in January 1923.

OWNER AND PHOTOGRAPHER CREDITS

Herewith Automobile Quarterly acknowledges grateful appreciation to the owners of automobiles and trucks featured in this book. Photographs are referenced by page number. All uncredited photographs are from private sources and the archives of Automobile Quarterly. Duplicate photographs are not available. Photographs may not be reproduced without permission.

Photographers are credited in the following manner: DLMV is Don Vorderman, LSB is L. Scott Bailey, RQ is Roy Query, RL is Rick Lenz, RAB is Richard A. Brown, WLB is William L. Bailey, HAC is Henry Austin Clark, Jr., DC is Dan Carter, SG is Stan Grayson, RB is Russ Berry, DO is Don Owens, BJ is Bud Juneau, SR is Stan Rosenthall, DH is Douglas Houston and JC is Josip Ciganovic.

PAGES 16–17: Oldsmobile factory, Courtesy of National Automotive History Collection.
PAGES 18–19: 1897 Oldsmobile, Smithsonian (LSB);
1902 Oldsmobile, Courtesy of Harrah's Automobile Collection;
1904 Oldsmobile, Courtesy of Tommy Protsman.
PAGES 20–21: 1912 Oldsmobile, Bud Ley (HAC);
1908 Oldsmobile, Oldsmobile Collection (LSB);
1910 Oldsmobile, (LSB).
PAGES 22–23: 1905 Buick, Alton Walker (RL);
1906 Buick, Jack Garrison (RL);
1910 Buick, Sloan Museum (LSB).
PAGES 24–25: 1918 Buick, Raymond LaPorte (RL);
1910 Buick, Harrah's Automobile Collection (RL);
1915 Buick, Robert Scott (RL).
PAGES 26–27: 1903 Cadillac, Pollack Automobile Collection (LSB);
1907 Cadillac Osceola, Pollack Automobile Collection (LSB);
1907 Cadillac Model K, J. Renzulli (RL).
PAGES 28–29: 1912 Cadillac, Harrah's Automobile Collection (DLMV);

1913 Cadillac, Harrah's Automobile Collection (DLMV);
1915 Cadillac, Al Carroll (RL);
1916 Cadillac, Herb Sculnick (LSB).
PAGES 30–31: 1912 Oakland, Iver Hoerle (RL);
1911 Buick truck, Ed and Margaret Chatfield (RL).
PAGES 32–33: 1912 Chevrolet, Sloan Museum (DO);
1912 Little, Pinky Randall (RQ);
1914 Chevrolet Royal Mail, Pinky Randall (RQ);
1914 Chevrolet Baby Grand, Pinky Randall (RQ);
1917 Chevrolet, Tom Meleo (RL).
PAGES 34–35: Camshafts being fitted at Buick factory, Gerry Fauth;
Buick ambulance, Terry B. Dunham;
Buick tank, *The Flint Journal*;
Buick armored car, National Automotive History Collection.
PAGES 36–37: 1920 McLaughlin-Buick, Sloan Museum (LSB);
1920 Oldsmobile, Oldsmobile Collection (LSB);
1921 Oakland, Chuck Braswell (RL);
1921 Buick, Ronald W. Cook (WLB).
PAGES 38–39: 1923 Chevrolet, Henry Ford Museum (WLB);
1922 Buick, Frank A. Kleptz (RL);
1924 Buick, Lou Staller (SG).
PAGES 42–43: 1926 Buick, Gordon Dennis (RL);
1925 Cadillac, Mrs. G. Bauer (RL);
1926 Pontiac, Don Bougher (RL).
PAGES 44–45: 1927 Chevrolet truck, Don Hoying (RQ);
1928 Chevrolet truck, Harrah's Automotive Collection;
1926 Chevrolet truck, Scott M. Schondlmyer (RQ);
1927 Chevrolet station wagon, Calvin Jordan, Jr. (RQ).
PAGES 46–47: 1928 Cadillac, A.N. Rodway (RQ);
1929 LaSalle, A.N. Rodway (RB);
1927 LaSalle, Garth E. Carrier (RL).
PAGES 48–49: 1929 Oldsmobile, Kemp Browning (RL);
1928 Chevrolet, Thomas Coates (RQ);

1929 Pontiac, Robert and Harlene Rosenberg (RL).
PAGES 50–51: 1928 McLaughlin-Buick, Aubrey and Bernice Marshall (SR);
1928 Pontiac, A.N. Rodway (RB);
1928 Buick, Joseph Kotlar (DC);
1929 Chevrolet, Lew Clark (RQ).
PAGES 54–55: 1930 Vauxhall, A.N. Rodway (RB).
PAGES 58–59: 1930 V-16 engine, Rick Carroll (RQ);
1930 Cadillac, Rick Carroll (RQ);
1930 LaSalle, Jodie and Dick Kughn (RQ).
PAGES 60–61: 1930 Oakland, Wayne H. Weber (RL);
1930 Marquette, Richard Loveday (RL);
1930 Cadillac, Dave Towell (RL).
PAGES 62–63: 1931 Chevrolet, E. Munday (RQ);
1931 Oldsmobile, A.N. Rodway (RB);
1931 Buick, Don Allen (RL);
1931 Pontiac convertible, Automotive Classics, c/o Tommy Farrell (RL);
1931 Pontiac coupe, Lafe Harper (RL).
PAGES 68–69: 1932 Cadillac V-16, Maxwell Sapp (RL);
1932 Chevrolet, George Hornbostel (DLMV);
1932 Cadillac Series 355B, Dave Holls (LSB);
1932 Buick, David Crow (RL).
PAGES 70–71: 1933 Buick, Larry J. Havens (RL);
1933 Chevrolet, A.N. Rodway (RB);
1933 Pontiac, John W. Fobel (RL).
PAGES 72–73: 1934 Buick, Steve Qua (RL);
1934 Pontiac, Don Doten Pontiac, c/o Jim Botto (RL);
1934 LaSalle, Jodie and Dick Kughn (RQ);
1934 Cadillac, William T. Walter (RAB).
PAGES 74–75: 1934 Cadillac, J. Freeman (RQ).
PAGES 78–79: 1936 Buick, Nicola Bulgari (JC);
1936 Chevrolet, Robert Nadler (RL);
1935 Pontiac, Don Howell (RL).
PAGES 80–81: 1936 Chevrolet truck, C.J. Whitworth (RQ);
1935 Chevrolet, Perry H. Kremer (DLMV);
1936 Chevrolet, Roy Streval, Jr. (RQ).
PAGES 84–85: 1937 Chevrolet, Robert Nadler (RL);
1937 Oldsmobile, Oldsmobile Collection (LSB);
1937 Pontiac, William H. Eicher (RL);

BUILDING ON 75 YEARS OF EXCELLENCE